HAUNTED
BERWICK

Berwick-upon-Tweed, as seen from the old bridge.

HAUNTED
BERWICK

Darren W. Ritson

The
History
Press

To my wonderful partner Jayne Watson
and our beautiful daughter Abbey May Ritson

First published 2010

The History Press
The Mill, Brimscombe Port
Stroud, Gloucestershire, GL5 2QG
www.thehistorypress.co.uk

© Darren W. Ritson, 2010

The right of Darren W. Ritson to be identified as the Author
of this work has been asserted in accordance with the
Copyrights, Designs and Patents Act 1988.

British Library Cataloguing in Publication Data.
A catalogue record for this book is available from the British Library.

ISBN 978 0 7524 5548 8

Typesetting and origination by The History Press
Printed in Great Britain

Contents

About the Author

Darren W. Ritson is a civil servant and author who has studied ghosts and legends for over twenty years. He is a member of the Incorporated Society of Psychical Research and regularly contributes articles to *Paranormal* magazine, among others. His previously published works include *The South Shields Poltergeist: One Family's Fight Against an Invisible Intruder*, *Haunted Durham* and *Haunted Newcastle*. He lives in North Tyneside.

Also by the Author

Ghosts at Christmas

Haunted Durham

Haunted Newcastle

The South Shields Poltergeist: One Family's Fight Against an Invisible Intruder
(with Michael J. Hallowell)

Acknowledgements

Thanks to fellow researcher and writer Michael J. Hallowell for his endless help, support and guidance.

Massive thanks must go to fellow researcher and writer Rob Kirkup for allowing me to reproduce certain extracts from his book *Ghostly Northumberland*, along with some historical data, and for help with a few ghost tales that are featured herein that I was hitherto unaware of. To author Derek Dodds, and Pen & Sword Publishing, for allowing me to reproduce an extract from Derek's book *Northumbria at War*. To Julie Olley for providing illustrations for this volume; Suzanne Hitchinson for allowing the story of the haunted house that she investigated to be published herein; Derek Sharman of the Berwick Tourist Tours for sharing information regarding Halidon Hill. Special thanks must go to Paul Angus of the Red Lion Inn at Spittal, and Eddie and Sheila MacDonald of Main Street, Spittal, for telling me about the Galleon public house. My gratitude also goes to everyone that I spoke to and gleaned information from during the compilation of this book, without your tales and anecdotes this book may never have been written.

All pictures in this book were taken by Darren W. Ritson except where otherwise stated. Pictures of Edward Longshanks, the vampire's grave and Sawney Bean were taken from Wikipedia, where they are available to use copyright free.

Introduction

Berwick-upon-Tweed is the most northerly of English towns and is no more than a mile or two from Scotland. The quaint and aged market town of Berwick-upon-Tweed has been known to be 'too north for England, and too south for Scotland'. It is nicely tucked away in the far north-eastern corner of Northumbria, and is a place where the author has spent many a joyous day simply meandering around, and generally soaking up its wonderful historic and ambient feel. On many occasions I have been on the express bus from my home town of Newcastle-upon-Tyne, thundering my way up the picturesque coastal route, passing through historic places like Warkworth, Alnwick, Craster, Bamburgh and Lindisfarne. With a bag full of sandwiches and my trusty camera at the ready, I have eagerly awaited my arrival at this ancient walled town. I remember as a child visiting Berwick-upon-Tweed for 'days out' with my family during my school holidays. We stayed in a caravan just over the borders in a village called Coldingham, near St Abbs Head, and for day trips we visited places such as Edinburgh, Eyemouth, and of course Berwick. Maybe this is why I have such an affinity with the borders and Scotland; the memories I have of them are treasured ones and I always relish the opportunity to return to these breathtaking places.

My latest visit – during the researching and compiling of this book – was in the blustery autumn of October 2009. I took great pleasure in exploring the side streets and back alleys, the nooks and crannies that so remind me of other old-world towns and cities such as Durham and Newcastle. Personally, I find that Berwick-upon-Tweed has a lot more in common with other seaside villages, remarkable cities and ancient walled towns than most people realise.

A view of Berwick and the Tweed Estuary from the Spittal area of Tweedmouth.

You learn something new every day, so they say, and on one pleasant afternoon during a trip to Berwick in October 2008, I found out that the acclaimed artist, Laurence Stephen Lowry (1887-1976), also spent many a blissful hour in Berwick-upon-Tweed. But, instead of relentlessly sauntering around the streets of Berwick, as this author does, Lowry immortalised them on canvas.

In fact, Lowry painted so many Berwick-upon-Tweed locations that there is now a Lowry trail for the visitor to Berwick to follow. I came across dozens of side streets, and other parts of the town, where there are printed copies of his work mounted on the walls in glass frames, next to the very area that he painted.

It is believed that Lowry's first painting of Berwick was back in 1935, and, along with at least four other pictures, it was included in his first one-man exhibition in London in 1939. Lowry was so charmed with Berwick-upon-Tweed that he continued to visit the town for the rest of his life, and it is believed that Berwick-upon-Tweed inspired some of his finest works of art. Lowry, by all accounts, was also particularly interested in the way Berwick was enclosed by its magnificent town walls, as is the author. I have visited many towns across the UK, including York, London, Chester and Conwy in North Wales, where the town walls stand proud as a reminder of turbulent days gone by. Indeed, Newcastle-upon-Tyne (where the author was born and bred) is also a walled town and, like the other walled conurbations, Berwick-upon-Tweed's walls have their fair share of history … and the odd ghost story attached to them.

Berwick, unlike York, is not generally considered a 'haunted town', and with it being rather small you would be forgiven for thinking there cannot be many ghosts. Undeniably Berwick-upon-Tweed is in need of thorough researching regarding its spirits and hauntings; I hope that I have at least made a good start in this research process. I am led to believe that this is the first ever full book dedicated to Berwick's ghostly legends, and if so I am proud to have penned it. This wonderful coastal town is rich in history and has an abundance of character, charm, aesthetic beauty, and, not forgetting the odd ghost or two; the good folk of Berwick can be proud of their heritage.

An aerial view of Berwick-upon-Tweed taken in 1965. (Courtesy of Newcastle Libraries and Information Service)

I have personally uncovered a fair amount of ghost stories hitherto unknown to the general public. Of course, there are some tales of Berwick's ghouls which have previously been reported in books – hauntings that are quite well known to the town – but there is also a small collection of brand new accounts that were just waiting to be discovered. And let us remember that for all the ghost tales recounted in this volume, I can bet my bottom dollar there are just as many out there which are yet to be uncovered. If the reader knows of any Berwick ghost tales that are not featured in this book, whether they involve pubs, clubs, offices, shops, homes, parks, side streets or anywhere, then please do let me know as I would love to hear them. Please contact me on darren.ritson@blueyonder.co.uk.

Darren W. Ritson, 2010

A Short History of
Berwick-upon-Tweed

Berwick-upon-Tweed is an historic border market town that is now the most northerly town in England. It was founded during the time of the 'Kingdom of Northumbria', which was part of the seven Anglo-Saxon kingdoms of Great Britain during the Middle Ages. These Anglo-Saxon kingdoms – Wessex, Sussex, Kent, Essex, East Anglia, Mercia, and Northumbria – were known collectively as the Heptarchy. They eventually merged together to become the 'Kingdom of England', until all seven kingdoms simply came to be known as England.

The name 'Berwick' is actually of Norse origin and means heartland, or settlement of the bay. 'Ber' derives from *Bar*, which was a headland that cut across the Tweed; 'Wick' is said to come from either *Vik*, which meant bay, or *Wic* which meant settlement.

Berwick, upon the River Tweed, is in the far north-eastern reaches between Northumbria and Scotland. Its strategic location made it central to the ongoing and often bloody border wars between England and Scotland. Besieged and fought over, few towns in the UK have experienced such a turbulent past.

Between 1018 (some say 1147) and 1482, Berwick had been fought over, and had changed hands an incredible thirteen occasions. One of the most ferocious attacks on Berwick during these border wars came in 1296 and was led by Edward I of England. This subsequently led to the onset of the Scottish War of Independence.

It appears that King John Balliol had proclaimed his intentions to King Edward I by signing the 'Auld Alliance' with one of England's enemies, France. This was a declaration of war, so King Edward I decided to make Berwick an example and ordered that this small and innocent town should be ruthlessly destroyed, with

The Town Hall in Berwick's Marygate.

those standing in his way killed – in whatever fashion his soldiers chose. This barbaric slaughter of Berwick's citizens included almost every single man, woman and child. Rob Kirkup, in his book *Ghostly Northumberland*, recounts some of the action that occurred during that fateful onslaught:

> One bitterly cold winter morning a small group of farmers were working in the fields at first light when they saw English troops heading towards them. Before the farmers had a chance to react, they were hacked apart. It was nearing dawn when the soldiers arrived in Berwick town centre. Most people were still in bed asleep and they would never wake. The soldiers went from house to house killing everyone they found. It wasn't long before the town of Berwick was a scene of chaos and panic; families were trying to escape from their homes only to be met by armed solders who would cut down any living person they encountered. No one was spared; even toddlers and babies were murdered by the remorseless troops, loyal to their King. A group of locals made it as far as the low bridge, they were vastly outnumbered and they knew there was no way they would all escape. In order to give their children and women a chance of getting far enough from Berwick to be safe, the men agreed to stand and fight, although they knew that it meant they would all inevitably die. The small band of around 100 managed to kill an equal number of soldiers before they were overwhelmed and mercilessly hacked to pieces until the brave Berwick men were nothing more than a mass of blood and dismembered body parts. The total number murdered in the massacre of Berwick was almost 8,000 over two days.

Work then began on rebuilding the town, with new fortifications being constructed. Edward II continued this work after the demise of Longshanks and ordered the erection of a new defensive wall – a wall that would hopefully keep future invaders at bay. Large parts of this wall still stand to this day and can be seen by visitors to Berwick. In 1318, Robert Bruce captured Berwick and the town walls were modified and strengthened once more.

The walls of Berwick are some of the best preserved in the country and really are a sight to behold. I have often walked the length of these magnificent walls on cold and blustery days, wondering what it must have been like back in the days of vicious and bloody warfare.

One section of the wall, known as the Cumberland Bastion, is the area where a ghost soldier, thought to be one of the foot soldiers of Oliver Cromwell, has been seen dressed in seventeenth-century garb. Oliver Cromwell, prior to the Battle of Dunbar on 3 September 1650, mustered his forces at Berwick-upon-Tweed after marching through York, Durham and Newcastle. People who have seen the ghost claim that he silently walks the top of the Bastion until he is noticed, whereupon he withdraws a razor-sharp knife from his belt and cuts his own throat with it. As he falls to the ground he is said to slowly dissolve into thin air, leaving nothing but an eerie chill and somewhat frightened witnesses.

In the Castlegate area of the town is the Berwick Wall – very imposing walls located near the main car parking area next to the supermarket. These defences were built around Berwick between 1558 and 1570, primarily to protect Queen Elizabeth I and Protestant England from the Catholic Scots and their allies, the French. Berwick had been a walled town for over 250 years before these new defences were constructed; the old walls enclosed a much bigger town, including the area leading up Castlegate as far as the railway station. These new walls cut the town in two with the huge arch gate being the only way in and out. Originally, the gate was even narrower than it is today, with the gap being only one cart wide. Wooden doors, and a drawbridge over a moat, were used to keep people either in or out. At night the gates were closed and locked and no one was let through, which sometimes caused considerable problems. In *A History of Berwick-upon-Tweed*, dating back to 1799, Dr Fuller writes:

> If a person upon his first coming up to the gates quarrels with the guard, the greatest importunities will more than likely be of no avail. Even medical people returning from the country and though exhausted by fatigue and lack of sleep are sometimes detained for a long time at the gate. On such occasions, the sentry insists that the person is using a fictitious name and he will not even look to inform himself whether it is so or not.

A view of the old bridge or 'Berwick Bridge', and Berwick-upon-Tweed, taken from the Royal Tweed Bridge.

Above: *The impressive Elizabethan ramparts on a stormy autumnal day, perfect for ghost hunting.*

Right: *Edward I (Edward Longshanks).*

A painting of Berwick Castle and its town by J.M.W. Turner, c. 1600. (Courtesy of Newcastle Libraries and Information Service)

The guard's actions did have tragic consequences one night when two girls were sent to get help for a woman who was giving birth. They were not allowed through the gate and the help which was so desperately needed never came. This resulted in the death of both mother and child.

In 1018, the area of Northumberland that was north of the River Tweed was surrendered to Scotland after the Battle of Carham (also known as the Battle of Coldstream). Interestingly, Berwick-upon-Tweed was, for a time, known as South Berwick by the Scottish so that it could be differentiated from North Berwick, near Edinburgh.

By 1482 the town was captured for the final time by Richard, Duke of Gloucester, who went on to become King Richard III. Since then it has been governed by the English and in 1551 it was made into a county corporate. A county corporate was used for local government in England, Ireland and Wales, and was effectively a small self-governing county, normally covering cities or small towns that were deemed important enough to be independent from the counties. A county corporate could, in actual fact, be known as a county in its own right.

During the reign of Queen Elizabeth I, enormous amounts of money were invested in a massive project to reinforce and remodify Berwick's fortifications. Sadly, most of these magnificent defences were demolished in the 1800s but, fortunately for us, plenty still remain today – namely the army barracks and the impressive town walls, which are now looked after by English Heritage.

The Cumberland Bastion, where a ghost soldier has allegedly been seen vanishing into thin air.

Oddly, after 526 years, a Scottish MP made calls in Scottish parliament for Berwick to become, once more, an official portion of Scotland. At least in 2008 it was done in a civil and humane manner, rather than the Scots thundering down the A1 and horribly butchering the townsfolk. On this occasion, the debate over Berwick was about getting better public services from the government. Although many people liked the idea of Berwick becoming Scottish (over 55 per cent of its townsfolk), the transition never happened. However, in 2009 the Borough of Berwick-upon-Tweed was abolished, and all of its councils and functions were transferred to Northumberland County Council.

A thriving border market town, rich in history, Berwick is a wonderful place to live and holiday. It is a place that I never become tired of visiting. The fact that its folklore and ghost legends have never been documented in one collection has made my recent trips here all the more fascinating; you hold in your hands the culmination of many months of hard work and research. I hope you enjoy this book as much as I have enjoyed visiting, researching and uncovering the wealth of ghost stories that Berwick-upon-Tweed has to offer.

one

The Ghosts of Berwick-upon-Tweed

Berwick Castle

The castle that was once the home to so many English and Scottish kings was situated on the site now occupied by Berwick railway station; however, there are small sections of the one-time fortress that still remain today. Originally, the Scottish King David I built the castle. King David I, a twelfth-century ruler, was known as the Prince of the Cumbrians and reigned as king between 1124 and 1153. Not only did he build Berwick's great fortress, he made the township of Berwick one of the four royal burghs of Scotland. This, essentially, allowed the town's freemen certain privileges and rights, which up until that point they were not privy to.

A burgh was an independent mutual body in Scotland and was normally a township. These burghs had been in existence since the twelfth century, but nowadays they have nothing more than ceremonial value. In 1975 the burgh status was abolished and only two still exist, if only by name of course, and they are *Edinburgh* and *Roxburgh*.

Berwick's great castle was rebuilt and modified by Edward I (1239-1307) following the great siege of Berwick in 1296. Edward I, known as Longshanks due to his great height, was also known – by some – as the 'Hammer of Scots'. He achieved his infamous historical reputation by conquering many parts of Wales before he meted out the same treatment on the Scots. Edward Longshanks reigned as king from 1272 until his death in 1307 whereupon his son, Edward II, succeeded him. Edward II was nothing like his father. Longshanks was a brave, courageous and successful king who took part in many ferocious battles; his successor's reign was nothing short of a catastrophe, with military defeats, political backbiting and total incompetence.

Berwick railway station, c. 1910. (Courtesy of Newcastle Libraries and Information Service)

This great siege of 1296 saw Edward I capture Berwick, which subsequently led to the onset of the Scottish War of Independence. Derek Dodds, in his book *Northumbria at War*, discusses this act of violence in great detail:

> Newcastle was thronged with the northern levy as they prepared to snatch Berwick from Scottish hands. It was taken back with the utmost ferocity. The iron-capped English footmen scythed down Berwick's wretched townsfolk without compassion until ordered to stop by Edward himself. With a clash and a spark of steel which would resonate through Northumberland, 'Longshanks' had struck the first cruel blow in a titanic Anglo-Scottish war.

What must it have been like to be there, one wonders. As the Berwick townsfolk were mercilessly butchered in their homes and streets, with nowhere to escape, and the slaughtered and decapitated corpses filled the cobbled streets with warm blood, the agonising screams of these unfortunate victims of an ancient feud would have echoed throughout the land like never before. It must have been horrendous.

It was after this atrocity that the castle was modified and rebuilt. With walls as high as 50ft (15m), and 12ft (4m) thick, the castle really was an impressive edifice, standing on a natural rock outcrop that dominated the surrounding township and the River Tweed. With steep valleys either side of it, strategically it was one of the best-placed castles in the land. Because of this, you would think that the castle would not have been seized many more times. But it was.

As aforementioned, both the castle and its township were subjected to many conflicts between the Scottish and English empires. The strong position of the castle made the task of attacking it a rather difficult one, so different methods and approaches were adopted in order to successfully capture it. Armies would often lay siege, resulting in the bloodshed of many Scottish and English soldiers. On other occasions more peaceful means were employed and guards were bribed. In 1318, King Edward II and his men used a device called the 'sow', which was essentially a portable wooden shelter. This sow was used as a safe haven as they worked under the walls in an effort to weaken the defences. But the Scots were one step ahead. They had somehow become aware of the sow and devised a machine that dropped enormous bricks and rocks upon it while the English were sheltered underneath. The bricks and rocks shattered the wooden sow, killing the English and ultimately preventing them from capturing the castle, this time.

Berwick railway station today. The building you see here is said to be on the site of the former castle's Great Hall.

An image of the ruined Berwick Castle. Note its strategic position high on the hilltop. (Courtesy of Newcastle Libraries and Information Service)

This 'rock dropper' was invented and built by a man named John Crabbe, who was an Aberdeen-based pirate. In 1332 he was captured by the English and given an ultimatum. He could either work with the English army, as he had skills that were simply too valuable to lose, or face death. It was not a difficult choice and he decided to work for the English. He returned to Berwick in 1333, helping Edward III recapture the town in the process, and went on to serve England in the continuing wars with Scotland and France, before dying comfortably and respectably in 1352.

In the later stages of the castle's history, the ruins were said to have been used as a sort of quarry, which provided stones for the nearby Berwick Barracks and the Royal Border Bridge. The ticket office and platform of the railway station is said to be where the castle's Great Hall once stood. The remaining wall that is known locally as 'the white wall' is the only standing remnant of the magnificent castle that once occupied this spot. This stretch of wall extends from the upper level of the station down the steep hill to the River Tweed. It guards a rather ominous flight of stone stairs known as 'Breakneck Stairs'.

The many arches of the magnificent Royal Border Bridge. Much of the former castle was used to build this structure.

Above: *An alternate view of one of the remaining walls of Berwick's impressive ruined castle. This section leads to Breakneck Stairs. (Courtesy of Newcastle Libraries and Information Service)*

Left: *An artist's impression of the ghost piper said to haunt Breakneck Stairs. (Picture by Julie Olley)*

For many years the ground in and around the location of the railway station and old castle had been soaked in English and Scottish blood. With so many grisly deaths taking place there, you would imagine this area to be extremely haunted. However, only one spectre is said to reside at Berwick Castle, despite all the deaths and butchery of bygone days. It is said that the phantom of a Scots piper can sometimes be seen, but he is more often heard as he patrols the ruined battlements, pacing up and down the aforementioned Breakneck Stairs. He is also said to haunt the ruined sections of the castle at the foot of the steep embankment near the river.

This raises the question of why a piper would ever have patrolled these areas. For this we have to look at the history of Scottish pipers and what role they played in the days of battles and sieges. What I discovered fascinated me and, had I not been researching this book, the chances of me learning this fact would have been slim. It appears that the bagpipes, or 'the pipes', were looked upon by the Scots as an instrument – in the sense of a battle tool, as well as a musical instrument – that essentially geared up the Scottish fighters whilst simultaneously putting the fear of God into their opponents by 'psyching' them out. It was a psychological aspect of the pre-battle build-up very similar to the Native Americans' method of screaming and whooping as they advanced forth on horseback. By all accounts, this method worked well for the Scots and the sound of the pipes reverberating through the Northumbrian air well and truly stirred the souls of the English; this was something they really feared.

We now know why the piper would have patrolled the battlements of the great castle, it only remains to be seen why he still haunts the place. The phantom piper may simply be a psychic or 'stone tape' recording of days gone by that is replayed repeatedly and will be forever more. Perhaps he is an historical figure who has been brought back to life by persistent folklorists, local legend and the desire to believe in such romantic tales – or maybe he really is the shade of a Scottish warrior who is still patrolling his beloved castle and town, just waiting for the next invasion from the English armies.

I asked the staff at Berwick train station if they had ever heard or seen the phantom piper of Berwick Castle, and was told 'no', although some staff had heard the legend. A grey-headed member of staff, with a wonderful disposition, informed me that the last time the piper was spotted was allegedly back in the early 1970s by an Edinburgh man who was passing through Berwick on business.

The Bell Tower

The Bell Tower is a small section of the Berwick fortifications that is situated in the north-west area of the town along Northumberland Avenue. The Bell Tower is not actually the original but an Elizabethan replacement; its rounded base is medieval. One can only speculate as to why the original tower was demolished. Perhaps it was destroyed during one of the many sieges, or perhaps the edifice was deemed unsafe due to many years of punishment from the cold North Sea winds and rains which batter the mainland with such ferocity. Who knows?

Perched in the centre of a long grassy knoll, this small octagonal tower, which was built 700 years ago, still – albeit silently nowadays – keeps watch over Berwick's medieval walls and township. When I first stood at the base of this monumental edifice, looking up at it from the ground, I couldn't help but be taken aback by its presence there.

It is here where I was told by one of the locals about strange and eerie noises that emanate from inside the old tower on windy nights. A rather pleasant, middle-aged lady, who was out walking her dogs, approached me and asked, 'Why the interest in the tower?' I got the impression that she saw me photographing it and sensed my admiration. I must admit it was nice to be approached for a change, as opposed to me pestering other folk, asking them questions and attempting to gain details about potential ghosts.

According to my informant, who chose not to be named, 'Some say the horrid screeches and wails are the screams of former Scottish soldiers that were once said to be kept housed in this vicinity after being captured; others say it is simply the wind as it howls through the ruined shell.' I would probably go with the latter, as the howling wind seems a lot more plausible than the cries of Scottish prisoners. The possibility remains, though, that there just might be some truth in these local beliefs.

What is more interesting is the mysterious sound of a tolling bell which rings out from time to time, usually on cold and misty mornings. I mentioned earlier that the tower silently keeps watch over Berwick's medieval walls and township.

The Bell Tower on Northumberland Avenue, c. 1920. Some Berwick folk claim the bell, which is now long gone, can still be heard to ring on cold, misty mornings. (Courtesy of Newcastle Libraries and Information Service)

But this is not strictly true if we are to believe the testimony of some of the local folk. I was informed that, every now and again, the sound of the bell that once rang out from this very tower is heard, warning the townsfolk of impending danger. Is it imagination? A made-up story? Is it perhaps the sound of another bell – its chimes carried from elsewhere by the wind? Or is it the ghostly chimes of a bell that once rang out from this ancient and well-used bell tower?

The tower is situated north of Berwick and this would have been the ideal location for a lookout and warning post. The bell was used, presumably, to warn the townsfolk of Berwick of impending attack from the Scots. One can only speculate as to why the tower now stands bell-free. My only conclusion is that it must have fallen into disrepair many years after the sieges and battles came to an end and, for health and safety reasons, it was brought down and perhaps placed in a museum.

Just a few metres down the road stands a ruined section of the sixteenth-century two-storey artillery tower, said to have been designed by Longshanks' father, King Henry III. Known as Lord Soulis Tower, or Lord's Mount, this circular former gun tower had enough room to house almost twelve cannons, with six being housed on the lower level, and another six on the upper level. There was room for accommodation there too with a kitchen and a water well. A captain's house also occupied this site, but when Berwick's famous Elizabethan ramparts were built in 1588, the captain's house became redundant. To my knowledge, there are no ghost stories linked to this site.

The Castle Hotel, Castlegate

The Castle Hotel stands at the top of Castlegate and is just opposite the railway station. This wonderful sixteen-bedroom hotel is a wonderful place to stay. It houses its very own restaurant, which is also open to non-residents. It also has a beautifully refurbished bar, complete with roaring log fires and comfortable armchairs for you sink into after sightseeing.

I often wondered, when passing the Castle Hotel, if it was haunted. I had heard that it may well be – but nothing was substantiated. On one of my many visits to Berwick – this time in the autumn of 2009, during the preparation of this book – I made it my business to venture into the hotel to enquire about any ghosts residing there. I wanted to know for certain if the hotel was haunted, and was rather astonished by what I was told.

The hotel, it seems, is where the acclaimed artist L.S. Lowry stayed during his trips to Berwick-upon-Tweed. During my visit there, I got chatting to the hotel owner, Donald Ringland, who very kindly told me about the hotel and its

The Castle Hotel on Castlegate. Renowned painter L.S. Lowry stayed here on his visits to Berwick.

one-time famous guest. He also showed me the very area in the lounge where L.S. Lowry would sit and relax – sometimes happily sketching on his pad. On one occasion he gave a member of staff a signed sketch, after doodling it in the lounge, and it went on to sell for thousands of pounds many years later.

Lowry's presence in the building is always felt, but it must be stressed that this is not in the usual sense. By this I mean that the building is not actually haunted by the ghost of Lowry, but his visits there have certainly left a mark upon the hotel. In a way the whole town of Berwick exudes an air of Lowry and wherever you go, while visiting this most wonderful of coastal towns, you are sure to be walking in the shadow of this famous artist. So, his 'spirit' does live on in Berwick, and of course at his favourite hotel, the Castle Hotel.

The Lions, Elizabethan Ramparts

L.S. Lowry spent so much time in Berwick that he once considered moving here. One magnificent house in particular, known as 'The Lions', was a potential home for the acclaimed artist after he spotted it in 1947 during one of his many visits to the area. The house, which dates from 1807, has sweeping views of Berwick from the top floors. It would have been an ideal location for Lowry to immortalise the views of the town he loved so much. As it happened, he never bought the house due to the levels of damp that it was suffering from at the time. Nowadays, the house is home to a number of flats, providing accommodation to four or five tenants.

The Lions is so named because of the two stone lions, sitting high upon stone plinths, guarding the residence from either side of the entrance gates. There is something distinctly sinister about these two beasts; they look, to me, more like Devil dogs that have came straight from the fiery depths of hell.

One of the magnificent yet demonic-looking stone lions that guard the The Lions.

The Lions. This was a potential home for the acclaimed artist L.S. Lowry after he spotted it during one of his many visits to the area in 1947.

Coxon's Tower

Coxon's Tower stands on the line of the medieval walls that were built to protect the town from naval attacks from the Scottish allies, the French. The Auld Alliance was a series of offensive and defensive treaties between the two countries that were solely aimed at the English. The first treaty to be signed was in Paris in 1295, and from that point on the Scots had an invaluable ally that could essentially assist in the capturing of Berwick. Not only could they attack from the north, their French allies could attack in unison with them from out at sea. The English knew this all too well and therefore had to make drastic changes in their defence systems.

The tower was originally known as the Bulwark in the Sands. It has a ribbed vault and a fourteenth-century lower chamber, which can be seen if you venture down the narrow steps by the path. It also has an upper gun deck, which was reconstructed in 1491. The author does not know why the gun deck was reconstructed, but can offer some suggestions. Perhaps work was carried out on the gun deck to make it

Looking down the stairwell from the top of Coxon's Tower.

bigger – surely having space for more weapons would prove quite valuable. This, in effect, would make the tower more powerful and therefore harder to penetrate. The thought occurs that the original deck may have been destroyed, and therefore the remaking of the tower was quite simply essential. Whatever the reason for its reconstruction, the fact remains that the second version was far more effective than the first.

From inside the walls the tower stands at about 12ft-high. From the riverside it is about 50ft-high, as are the rest of the magnificent ramparts that run alongside the river this way.

On one of my many visits to Berwick, on a blustery October day, I ventured down to the section of the ancient wall that faces out into the Tweed's mouth. Early that particular morning, I was up sharp and had ventured out to photograph the sun as it rose over the North Sea. By the time I returned back to my accommodation the weather had started to take a slight turn for the worse. The week in Berwick-upon-Tweed was a family holiday, with my intention being to spend some quality time with my partner and our daughter. However, discovering some new ghost stories during my visit was also an ulterior motive for me during our short getaway.

By mid-afternoon, and after a hearty pub lunch and a pint of real ale, we decided to take a walk around Berwick's perimeter. This took us down by the estuary and along the river, where the array of wildlife was a joy to behold. By the time we reached Coxon's Tower, the autumn leaves were blowing everywhere and strong gusts of wind were howling trough the trees, bending them over almost to a 45° angle. The skies were dark and gloomy, and it looked as though a thunderstorm was looming. No one else was around at that time and, for me, the weather conditions were perfect for investigating the ghosts that are said to haunt this area.

Less than an hour or so earlier, prior to walking around the town walls in this area, I had been chatting to a pub landlord who ran his alehouse in central Berwick. He informed me (upon my enquiries) that he had heard that Coxon's Tower had a ghost. He told me that the sound of a shouting man had been heard coming from inside the tower on occasion, but when people looked inside, or called out from the steps, no one answered. Of course no one can actually get inside the chamber as it is locked up with an old steel gate. The thought occurred to me that the sound of the shouting man could have been the wind howling through the apertures, creating this natural, but unnerving, phenomenon – similar to the wind howling through the orifices at the aforementioned Bell Tower.

Since I had my dictation machine with me (for my research notes), I decided to leave it recording inside the fourteenth-century lower chamber. If there was a ghost in there, perhaps he might oblige me with some sign, or perhaps even a message. I left the machine recording for fifteen minutes in total before returning to retrieve it. Upon picking up my machine, I hoped that I had been successful in my attempts to record something of a paranormal nature.

EVP recordings, or dictation device recordings, are, in my opinion, one of the best methods used in ghost hunting and I have personally had some amazing successes using this technique. However, one must be careful when analysing the results of such experiments as it can be so easy to misread, or misinterpret, the sound recordings you may get. On one occasion, I recorded an anomalous voice in a room at a venue in Durham City. There were only two people present in the room at the time and I know for a fact that these individuals (one being myself) never said the actual word that was recorded. The word in question was my name, 'DARREN', and was spoken in a male voice. Now, I wouldn't have been calling

Coxon's Tower is thought to be haunted by the sound of a 'shouting man' on stormy nights. Or is it just the wind as it howls through the apertures in the tower?

out my own name, and my companion at that time was a female! EVP sessions like these fascinate me, and it is why I always like to try the experiment when on my travels. You just never know what you might record. On this occasion, unfortunately, nothing of a paranormal nature was recorded.

The thought struck me that if there is a ghost residing in this small section of the wall, who on earth could it be, why does he shout so, and why would he be haunting the tower? One suggestion is that the ghost (if there is one) could be that of a former soldier who once defended this old town from the marauders. Having said that, the ghost could be absolutely anybody, couldn't he? Perhaps there is a normal explanation after all for these anomalous sounds.

Until more accounts of paranormal activity is reported, it will remain unclear whether there really is a ghost at Coxon's Tower, or whether it is nothing more than an uncorroborated anecdote.

The Battle of Halidon Hill

During my research for this book I made many visits to Berwick. On one trip, I was curious to find out more about the battles and sieges that have taken place in abundance in this war-torn historical region. Where there are ancient battlefields, there are sure to be ancient battlefield ghosts – so they say. The closest battlefield to Berwick-upon-Tweed is situated on the sloping hillsides a mile or so north-west of Berwick itself. The conflict that once took place there was known as the Battle of Halidon Hill.

I began my search at the local tourist information centre, in the hope of acquiring a leaflet, a book, or some form of literature about the battlefield and its history. I ended up getting a great deal more than I expected. In the shop was an important-looking local man dressed in National Trust greens. This chap, Derek Sharman, was the official tour guide of Berwick and, as it happened, he was about to embark on a tour of the town with a group of eager holidaymakers. Had I strolled in ten minutes later I would have missed him altogether but, as luck would have it, I managed to chat with him before he was due to leave on his 90-minute tour.

During the course of our conversation I attempted to glean some information about the Battle of Halidon Hill. Derek was very accommodating and quite happy to tell me all about the battle. He said:

The Battle of Halidon Hill was fought on 19 July 1333 between Edward III of England, and Lord Douglas of Scotland. It was, and still is, known as the Great Siege at Berwick

Berwick-upon-Tweed as viewed from the former battlefield known as 'Halidon Hill'. Fought on 19 July 1333, many men lost their lives here on this, the longest and most bitterly fought battle in the Berwick area. (Courtesy of Newcastle Libraries and Information Service)

as it was the longest and most bitterly fought battle in the Berwick area. For about twenty years or so after the Battle of Bannockburn, where Robert the Bruce defeated the English on 24 June 1314, the Scots had the upper hand so to speak and they were constantly marauding over England. At this time, the English had a useless king on the throne (Edward II) who did nothing whatsoever to protect the north of England. By 1333 England had a new king (Edward III) and he came north to besiege Berwick. This siege went on for three months and was the first siege in Britain that had cannons used as weapons. Towards the end of the siege the Scots sent a relief force to try and break their way through the surrounding English, by which time the English were occupying Halidon Hill. Their position there strategically covered the northern approaches to the town and the approaches from along the Tweed valley, so the Scots literally had to break through these defences in order to break the siege. With boggy marshland and swamps at the foot of Halidon Hill, the Scots found this 'siege break' particularly hard, and they were ultimately slaughtered and driven off during their attempt to retake Halidon Hill. The next day Berwick was forced to surrender, yet again changing hands. Not only was the Battle of Halidon Hill the first of the great battles in Britain where cannons were used, it was also the battle where the longbow proved its worth.

I asked Derek if he could tell me about any of the ghosts that are said to haunt this blood-soaked terrain. He told me, 'Quite often the farmers and crofters in those areas find bits and pieces of old battle equipment on the land, and old bones have been dug up from time to time.' Although he didn't know of any particular ghost stories, he did declare that, 'There ought to be, because there are lots of dead people there!'

I could not find any first-hand accounts of alleged paranormal activity up at Halidon Hill, but I am aware of a couple of websites that claim it is haunted by the soldiers who fell there. One website claims that the sloping hills of this battle site have been subjected to the ghostly moans and groans of the dead warriors. Another states that the apparition of a ghost soldier has been spotted running around aimlessly at dusk. Whether or not these accounts are true is unverified. If there are any ghost sightings that so far have been unreported, or perhaps if you visit the battlefield and experience something odd for yourself, please feel free to contact me and tell me all about it.

The *Berwick Advertiser*

The street known as Marygate is probably Berwick's most well-known area. At the foot stands the magnificent Town Hall and its famous spire, which can be seen from just about anywhere in the town. At the top, where it meets Castlegate, stands the imposing 'Cumberland Bastion', just one of the many impressive sections of Berwick's remaining town walls. Twice weekly Berwick hosts its traditional-style market there (Wednesdays and Saturdays) with stallholders selling their own home-grown local produce and much more. Meandering around the marketplace on a sunny day, perusing the stalls in search of a bargain or two, is a wonderful experience.

Located at 90 Marygate, set way back from the main road and opposite Golden Square, is the *Berwick Advertiser* building. I decided to pop in one day in the hope of acquiring some ghost stories that might have featured in their newspaper at some point. As I entered the building, I turned right through a door and then went straight ahead to where the main desk was situated.

I told the members of staff behind the counter who I was and explained that I was looking for spooky tales as part of my research. Before I had a chance to enquire about any ghost stories archived away in their records, the girls behind the counter exclaimed, 'Ghosts? There is a ghost in here.'

Of course, being informed of an alleged ghost in their premises delighted me, and I decided to enquire further. During our chat, a gentleman in a dark uniform (a security guard who I subsequently found out was called Michael) approached the counter and told me that he had experienced the ghost himself while in the building alone. He went on to say:

The Berwick Advertiser *building at No. 90 Marygate, believed by the staff that work there to be haunted by a former blacksmith called Joe.*

Upstairs there was an old work area; it isn't there now but it was once part of the building, and I was told a blacksmith used it. There used to be an old guy that once worked on these premises and he was called Joe Blythe. He had worked here for many years, and even lived on the premises. He had worked here for so long he was almost part of the building's fabric, and when I started here, over thirty years ago, he was even here then. However, not long after I began working here, Joe sadly died, and it is his ghost that is said to haunt this building. His presence is often felt here by the staff and on one night while in the building alone, I am sure that I actually heard him.

'What did you hear?' I asked Michael.

'Just a voice,' he replied.

'What did it say, then?' I pressed.

'I don't know. If I have to be honest, it was just one of those voices you hear and you don't understand what was being said, if you know what I mean? I was in the building alone and it came from inside one of the small corridors on the upper levels.'

'So what did you make of it?' I asked.

'Well, I was one of the most sceptical and cynical people, but I am now convinced that there is something in this. I know it was Joe; don't ask me how, I just know it was him.'

I explained to Michael and the girls behind the counter that it sounded like a classic case of someone loving the building so much that they wanted to continue residing there even after passing into the next world.

I then asked the girls if they had experienced anything while working in the building.

'No, and if I did I wouldn't be working here,' one said. I got the impression that this particular girl was an absolute believer and would be scared easily. And, as she would leave her employment if she experienced anything otherworldly, let's hope she doesn't!

Another lady vouched forth and explained to me that, on occasion, when she was in the building with only a few other people around, strange things had occurred. She told me that, every now and again, she had felt really cold when the heating was on full and all of the windows were closed. She also told me that on one occasion she heard a door close in one of the rooms upstairs, followed by the sound of footsteps across the floor. This startled her somewhat because she knew there was nobody up there.

Of course, human testimony is not always sound and one should always be aware that sometimes what people *think* they experience is completely different from what they *really* experience. For example, if a person imagines that there is a ghost in the premises where they work, then cold draughts and everyday noises such as creaks, coughs, and even noise pollution from outside the building, could be construed as paranormal. This, understandably, could exacerbate the fear factor for the individual concerned – especially if they are alone at the time. The heart rate begins to speed up, there is a rush of adrenalin, and soon other naturally-occurring sounds and commonplace incidents will become horribly misinterpreted. Small details that seem trivial to the witness, but are essential to the researcher, can be left out or forgotten, and at the same time new details may be subconsciously added to the narrative. I once heard someone say, 'The ghost story gets better each time it is told.' This is something that every researcher should bear in mind.

Has this happened at the *Berwick Advertiser* offices? Or is there a real spectre residing in the upper levels of the old building? Michael and the girls seem pretty adamant that there is, and even seem to know the ghost's identity. Maybe a scientific investigation of the building would shed some light on the matter. Either way, the staff are pretty sure that the ghost of Joe haunts the building. Perhaps he does, but we will never know for sure.

The Town Hall

The Georgian Town Hall is one of Berwick's most famous landmarks and its spire can be seen from miles away as it towers 150ft upwards, dominating the Berwick skyline. The Town Hall is situated at the foot of Marygate, where the street widens to accommodate the weekly markets and the annual May fairs. It was built in the 1750s by the Guild of Berwick, and was completed in 1761 when it became the centre for the municipal government and remained so for over one hundred years. The building comprises of the Guild Hall and town prison, which was built primarily for debtors and minor offenders. Escapes were quite common – a fact that was commented on by the Christian philanthropist and prison reformer Elizabeth Fry. Her 1819 report stated, 'nothing can be more defective than this small prison.' Elizabeth Fry was a major influence behind new laws that would make the treatment of inmates in the custody of Her Majesty more civilised. She was, in actual fact, supported in her efforts by the reigning monarch, Queen Victoria. For those interested, Elizabeth Fry has been depicted on the back of an English £5 note since 2002.

Many of L.S. Lowry's paintings were of the old Town Hall building, and it appears that he too was inspired by the magnificent edifice. The curfew bell still rings from the tower for fifteen minutes every night at eight o clock.

When I arrived at the Town Hall, I got chatting with two locals who worked in the Doolally teashop, located on the ground floor of the premises. They were outside having a cigarette break, so I asked if they knew anything about the prison cells inside the building. One of the two, a young man, told me that it had been a very small prison with only six holding cells on the upper levels. I asked him if it was reputed to be haunted and he replied that he had always been led to believe that the prison was haunted by some of the former prisoners. He went on to say:

> With Berwick being a harbour, or sea port, many folk visited, and during their time there done bad things. They were kept here in these cells and often died in there. You should speak to the caretaker as he will be able to tell you more.

I was now rather intrigued so I sought out the caretaker, wondering just what new information he could give me in regards to the alleged ghosts of the Town Hall prison. Would he be a sceptic, or would he be a believer – and would I be permitted to enter the cells for a look around, or would he just show me the door? I soon found out. A few yards down from where the Berwick stocks are kept is a door which leads into the Town Hall itself. I was informed that the caretaker would be here. I gave this door four or five thunderous raps and, after a minute or so went by, I knocked again; this time, from behind the door, I heard footsteps – someone was coming.

The Town Hall, and on the top floors – Berwick's old prison.

Inside the old prison building. (Courtesy of Newcastle Libraries and Information Service)

When the door opened I was greeted by a nice chap answering to the name of Michael Erriot, who confirmed that he was the building's caretaker. I then quizzed him about the ghosts of Berwick Town Hall. During our conversation, he informed me that despite the fact he didn't believe in ghosts, and had had no experiences of the paranormal while working at the Town Hall, he could verify that others had, in the past, experienced strange occurrences.

'Like what?' I asked him.

'Cell doors,' he said, 'would often be heard to slam closed, eerie footsteps have been heard on occasions, people that are on the lower levels of the building have reported strange disembodied voices that seemed to be coming from the old holding cell areas.'

Unfortunately, the seasonal tours of the building had finished for the year, so getting a glimpse inside the old prison was out of the question. I did discover, however, that on that forthcoming Halloween an all-night ghost hunt had been arranged by a few of the Berwick locals. One wonders if anything of a paranormal nature occurred.

The Town Hall and its 150ft-high spire, c. 1890. (Courtesy of Newcastle Libraries and Information Service)

Victoria Buildings

Victoria Buildings is a wonderful old edifice located on Bridge Street, very close to the original old bridge that spans the River Tweed from Tweedmouth, and stands at the foot of the very steep West Street. In fact, this building can be seen in Lowry's painting entitled 'Bridge End' and is on the front of the 'L.S. Lowry in Berwick' leaflet. During my adventures around Berwick, I came across the building, which is an old-fashioned convenient store, and thought to myself, 'this place must have a ghost'. Perhaps it was a ghost hunter's instinct. I often find that, when I am out on my travels, I see many old and interesting looking buildings and have a feeling about whether or not they have a ghost. I remember once when I was in Ayr, on the west coast of Scotland, I walked past an old building. I ventured in and enquired about 'any potential resident ghosts' and was informed that the place was indeed haunted – my hunch had proved right.

I ventured inside Victoria Buildings after deciding it was likely to be 'spooked out' and was greeted by two gentlemen. One thing must be pointed out to other would-be ghost hunters at this point: if you are out and about in search of ghosts, you must be wary of those who try to pull your leg – or, to put it bluntly, mock you! I came across one example here and left the premises not knowing if the building was indeed haunted or not.

When I walked in, I said 'Good morning' and then asked if there were any ghosts inside the building. One gentleman said, 'Oh yes, there are indeed', and the other said, 'No, of course there isn't.'

'Oh, there is,' the first chap insisted.

The other man shook his head and proceeded to get on with his work. I got the impression that he was a sceptic and regarded any believers as either deluded or plain stupid.

I asked the other chap to tell me about the ghosts.

'I see them every day in here, one in particular,' he said.

'Can you tell me about it?'

'Aye. Every time I go down the back, I turn the corner and I see a gentleman every morning and say "good morning" to him. It's near the old tunnel,' he said.

'Old tunnel? That sounds interesting,' I said.

'Come with me,' he said.

He proceeded to take me through the back shop, through a door, and along onto an old landing where there was a magnificent old wooden staircase leading up to the next level. Along the passageway, and halfway up the flight of stairs, was a beautiful stained-glass window depicting a woman in yellow holding a baby. The chap then told me to 'come this way'.

The road leading to 'Bridge End' and 'West Street' from old Berwick Bridge.

'Mind, it's pitch dark down here, be careful,' he said.

As we turned the corner he stopped and told me that here is where he says 'good morning' to one of the resident ghosts of Victoria Buildings. Further down, he showed me the tunnel entrance that leads all the way along Bridge Street to the Sandgate area of the town. I ventured into the tunnel and walked in quite a distance. I must admit that, by this point, I was becoming rather nervous. As I ventured further into the tunnel it became darker and darker, the atmosphere changing with every step that I took. A few odd thoughts ran through my mind. The first thing was my actual welfare; was I being lured into a trap to be kidnapped and maybe beaten to death? (It happens!) Another thought was who – or what – would I bump into whilst down there? I also wondered just how far down this tunnel I could actually go. Unfortunately, I had no torch with me, and because the staff don't venture into these parts of the building too often, they didn't either. We made our way back out of the tunnel and into the shop.

I then asked this gentleman if he was pulling my leg about the ghosts here. I told him I was quite serious and I didn't want anyone to 'take the mick'.

He then admitted that, 'If I saw a ghost I wouldn't be working here!'

The other man said, 'I told you he was pulling your leg!'

The two gentlemen I spoke to (who were very nice, albeit wind-up merchants) thought that the building wasn't haunted. They told me they had been working there for years and had experienced nothing untoward. Fair enough, but one has to consider the fact that people can sometimes live and work in haunted properties without experiencing any paranormal phenomena at all – they may just not be 'in tune' with other planes of existence. Without carrying out scientific tests I cannot say for sure whether or not the building is haunted. I include this account to highlight the fact that there are people out there who will attempt to mislead researchers who enquire about such matters.

I had a chat with William Cowe, the fellow who owns Victoria Buildings, and he told me that it houses no ghosts. I enquired about bringing in a research team to investigate the premises (to carry out a diagnostic investigation) but was politely

William Cowe & Sons; home of the original Berwick cockles, c. 1920. The building to the left (across the cobbled embankment), is Victoria Buildings, where the author had a very interesting tour of the underground cellars and tunnel.

refused overnight access. However, I am still fascinated by the tunnel. Those who study ghost lore will be aware that ghost tales often centre on buildings with mysterious tunnels which more often than not connect with other locations nearby. Borley in Essex, the Hellfire Caves in Buckinghamshire, Clifton Hall and Dover Castle are a few good examples.

Tunnels, it seems, attract ghosts, and wherever there are tunnels there are stories. If there are no ghosts at Victoria Buildings, or in its hidden underground passageway, there is still a fabulous air of mystery. Why is the tunnel there? What purpose did (or does) it serve? Where exactly in Sandgate does it lead? And what tales does it have to tell?

The Bridge Street Morgue

This particular story was relayed to me during my visit to the aforementioned Victoria Buildings. While chatting with William Cowe, he said, 'I don't think that my buildings are haunted but I do know of one or two ghosts that are said to reside here in Berwick.' I was very much intrigued by this and asked him if he could kindly elaborate.

One story concerned a former employee of his whose husband, a builder, was working on the old morgue/mortuary building that once stood along Bridge Street. One day, while at work, this individual suddenly became conscious of a strange presence close by. It's amazing how many times this 'sense of presence' is felt by unsuspecting people. There is a theory to suggest that it can happen to anyone at any time as we can all pick up on things on a subconscious level. It has even happened to this author while visiting the Schooner Hotel in Alnmouth on the Northumberland coast. That particular encounter ended in a gashed wrist, a stubbed toe, a bump on the head and a smashed clipboard after I ran headlong into a wall trying to get away. This is one of the only times I have ever panicked in a haunted location, and by Jove did it scare me witless. If it has ever happened to you, perhaps you can relate to the worker in the morgue.

The air around him is reported to have suddenly gone ice-cold, and a sense of apprehension enveloped him. The worker knew he was on his own in that particular area, but had presumed that someone – perhaps another construction worker – had come to see him. He was mistaken, for when he turned round a gaunt-looking, balding old man, who appeared to be wrapped up in a white blanket, stood there staring at him in a rather menacing manner. The worker froze on the spot and stared back at this rather frightening vision. Then the old man faded into the ether right in front of the construction worker's eyes. At this point,

An artist's impression of the balding ghost said to haunt the old Bridge Street morgue. (Picture by Julie Olley)

the man dropped his tools and ran from the building. I know from experience that witnessing something supernatural can be a harrowing ordeal, and some people even end up with serious trauma.

Although this report is third-hand (I would have favoured a first-hand account) it was told to me in good faith.

Sawney Bean and the Legend of the Borderland Cannibals

If you went back to the sixteenth century and mentioned the name Sawney Bean, the reaction you would receive would be that of tremendous anger and/or apprehension. You would also no doubt sense the utter fear spawned at the mere whisper of his name, for Sawney (Alexander) Bean was the loathsome leader of a large horde of mass murderers and cannibalistic criminals who sent spine-chilling dread through ancient Scotland.

Or did he? There are people who suggest that the legend of Sawney Bean is just that, a legend. His supposed execution for the murders and subsequent cannibalisation of over 1,000 people perhaps never happened, as no records exist that can accurately document it. There is, however, a story that appeared in the old crime catalogue of Newgate Prison in London, which documents some activities of this nature. It is from this catalogue, the Newgate Calendar, that the stories may have originated. It is said, however, that these journals and documents were highly embellished, and were drawn from other unknown and unreliable sources. Nowadays, most historians tend to consider the fearful murderous man-eater a myth, although his chronicles have become legendary.

Alexander Bean was thought to have been born in East Lothian some time in the sixteenth century and is said to have worked with his father until he decided that an honest working life was not for him. He wanted to live life on the edge, to experience thrills, spills and excitement. To do this he decided to live a life of crime and so left home with a lady friend who shared his attitude. The pair – it is thought – ended up living in a cavern down by the sea in what is now Ayrshire, on the west coast of Scotland. By all accounts it was a deep cavern which sloped upwards, therefore when the tide came in it actually blocked the entrance without flooding the back of the cave. They lived there for almost twenty-five years.

During their occupation of the cave, the pair bore many children and those children also procreated. Orgies among the siblings were said to have been commonplace, resulting in many inbred children. Overall there is said to have been forty-eight members of the Sawney Bean crew, all of whom were members of the same family. They survived by robbing people in night-time waylays and ambushes. The bodies of their victims were said to have been brought back to the cave where they were dismembered and then devoured by the murderous inbreds.

Body parts were sometimes washed from their hideaway with the outgoing tides, and turned up on the nearby shore. This caught the attention of the local authorities, as did the growing number of individuals who were being reported missing. Since the Bean clan were so secretive, and worked at night, nothing was done to stop the atrocities, although attempts were made.

Eventually it was decided that something must be done about the problem, and a number or organised searches were subsequently carried out. During one of these investigations the cave was discovered; it occurred to the searchers that it might be a hideaway. When the tide came in, however, they decided that no one could possibly be living in such a dark, cold and watery hollow, so it was not fully explored. People kept on disappearing and body parts continued to be found on nearby shores. So, in a desperate act of frustration, it is said that some local people were held responsible for the murders and were rounded up, then publicly strung up; but still the disappearances occurred, indicating that the authorities were getting it all wrong.

The tale of Sawney Bean and his hunger for human flesh is primarily centred around Scotland's west coast, namely Ayrshire. However, being born and bred in East Lothian, it is not hard to imagine that he may have frequented the east coast of Scotland, and perhaps the far reaches of north-east England – perhaps even Berwickshire. Some authors believe this to be the case and there are stories to support the theory.

There are at least two versions that I can find of one such tale; they both involve a married couple who were travelling on horseback. The first account suggests that they had been recently married at York, and were travelling home through Northumberland and Berwick to head towards the borders, when they were unexpectedly accosted by Sawney Bean and his crew. The man, being accustomed to warfare and having his weapons with him, fought off some of the gang until a group of local fairground-goers came to the couple's rescue and helped to see off the cannibals. Unfortunately, his wife was pulled from the steed and killed in the fracas.

The second account suggests that the couple had been to a local fair. As with the other version of events, the lady in question was allegedly dragged off the horse. However, in this tale it is claimed that she was ripped open by a single blow to the stomach with an axe wielded by one of Bean's crew, whereupon they dived face-first into the gaping wound and ripped her bloody innards with their rotten black teeth. They then approached the man on his horse but, as they did, the horse galloped off in a frenzy, throwing the rider from its back. Luckily for him, his lower leg was caught in the saddle and he was left dangling, upside-down, as the horse galloped away. The Bean crew were left further and further behind as the horse ran into the distance; the man had escaped.

Regardless of which story is true (if either), this was the alleged turning point in the Sawney Bean saga, as people now knew who was responsible for the missing folk

An image depicting the ruthless cannibal known as Sawney Bean. Most legends tell the story of Sawney Bean taking place on the west coast of Scotland near Ayrshire, but not all. Some suggest it was the rocky coastline of Berwickshire where he prayed on innocent people, killing them before eating them raw.

and the human remains that were turning up on the beaches. With Bean's activities now known to all and sundry, something at last could be done to stop him.

Once the king heard about these events, he decided to lead a manhunt with over 500 of his men and some blood-hungry dogs. The previously overlooked cave was subsequently searched and was found to be the den of the Bean crew. Bones, and the remains of rotting humans, were found strewn about the caves. The stench was so appalling it was considered inconceivable that locals had not noticed anything, as the smell surely would have been carried on the sea breezes and drifted across the land.

The Bean crew were eventually captured and taken in chains to Edinburgh, where they were sentenced to death – without trial! Their crimes were considered so appalling, so despicable, so heinous, that they were disposed of quickly; but not before a good torturing first. The men had their genitals savagely removed, along with their hands and feet; they were then left to bleed to death. The women and youngsters were made to watch their menfolk die, before they themselves were burned alive.

And so came the end of a terrible and lengthy reign of terror for the good folk of Ayrshire (or Berwickshire, depending on which version you prefer) and the blood-curdling fear of being eaten alive was felt no more. Sawney Bean and his crew were gone at long last, but his ghostly presence is said to have lingered on for many years to come. There was always the troublesome thought that in death he may have evaded his punishment and somehow, from beyond, he was free again to hound and feast upon the bodies of the innocent. His angry and restless spirit is said to have returned from the hell into which he was cast, to seek vengeance on those who brought his terrifying reign to such a torturous and gruesome end.

The Berwick Vampire (1)

I wrote a book on ghosts, published in 2009, entitled *Supernatural North*. This featured a short chapter on the ghosts of Berwick-upon-Tweed and included a harrowing account of an alleged vampire that had been terrorising the townsfolk in the 1700s. When I was researching material for this book, I discovered by chance that there were actually three macabre vampire tales relating to this ancient seaside town. When it comes to ghost lore, more often than not tales become interwoven with other tales, creating accounts that can differ greatly to the original. Ghost stories can be elaborated on, and exaggerated, and vital parts of the tale are somehow left out. Upon getting my teeth stuck into this story (sorry, I couldn't resist) I became aware of the three different vampire accounts, two that are very similar and one that is divergent.

Fellow researcher and writer on ghost lore Rob Kirkup released a book in 2008 entitled *Ghostly Northumberland*, which is a fascinating look at ghosts and hauntings in the Northumbria region. From Berwick to Bamburgh, from Dunstanburgh to Dilston, Rob takes the reader on a haunted tour of the county that will delight every paranormal enthusiast. It was while reading this book that I came across the second story regarding Berwick's vampire population. The story of the vampire that I originally heard – and wrote about in *Supernatural North* – follows this new account in the present volume. The third account comes courtesy of the acclaimed writer and expert on ghost lore Elliot O'Donnell. I contacted Rob Kirkup and asked if I could reproduce his account from *Ghostly Northumberland*. He very kindly allowed me to publish it verbatim:

In the early 1900s Betty Hough was happily engaged to Colin McFaddon, a farmer. They were very much in love and Colin saved every penny he earned so he could afford to marry Betty. They met every weekend at a local public house, their routine was always the same – they would have a drink and a sing song, and then upon leaving they would head to the barn at Colin's farm to make love in the hay.

One fateful Friday night at the public house, Betty excused herself and headed outside to the outdoor netty, a primitive toilet consisting of a plank with a hole in it in a small wooden hut. Colin began to get worried when Betty had been away ten minutes. A couple of women came into the bar saying that they'd been waiting to use the toilet, but the door was locked and the person inside wasn't answering when they had asked if everything was all right. Colin began to panic; he went outside and charged the door with his shoulder. Betty was still sat on the plank, but she was dead. Her neck had been ripped open and blood was still gushing from the wound.

This was the most exciting thing to happen in Berwick in years, and word quickly spread, many people believing that there was a vampire in Berwick and it was only a matter of time before it took another life. Colin was understandably devastated, even more so when he heard a rumour that Betty had been working as a prostitute in order to earn some more money to put towards their wedding. Colin McFaddon made a promise to track down her killer and bring them to justice.

Farm animals across Berwick were being mysteriously killed at night, bite marks being found and the animals seeming to have been drained of their blood. This strengthened the vampire theory and the majority of the locals were beginning to accept that this was indeed the case.

A few weeks later a 16-year-old girl was out picking brambles from a farm track. With the town fearful of another vampire attack, the girl's mother had told her to be home before dusk. However, she had lost track of time and dusk was upon her. She started to make her way home when she saw a dark figure up ahead walking towards her, a tall man of well over six feet, dressed in dirty clothes. As they passed each other the man turned around and jumped on the young girl. As she lay on her back with this man on top of her he opened his mouth to display two extremely large canine teeth, resembling fangs, he tried to bite her and grabbed at her as she screamed out. Two farmers heard the screams and rushed to the girl's aid. They wrestled the huge man to the ground and managed to restrain him. The man was taken to the magistrate who said that the man was not a vampire, but he was a madman and would face trial for the attempted rape of the young girl.

As he was being led away he bit one guard's throat out and made his escape as the other guards looked on in horror. Sniffer dogs were brought out and quickly picked up a scent. Colin McFaddon had been told about this man resembling a vampire and was convinced that this was the killer of his beloved Betty. He rounded up some of the locals keen to rid Berwick of the vampire, and they joined the hunt.

The scent led into woodland and a small makeshift camp with the remnants of a fire and a number of small dead animals – dogs, cats, and rabbits, appearing to be drained of their blood. Next to a huge tree was a large hole leading underground, this was where the man's scent ended. One of the men put their arms down the hole and felt a foot, leaping back in horror. Colin led the angry mob in for the kill. The dozen or so men quickly dug down and reached the escaped rapist. The guards were putting the man under arrest but Colin had other ideas, this man had killed his wife-to-be, and he shouldn't be allowed to live. Colin swung his shovel at the man, almost completely severing his head. Others started slashing out at the man, beating him to the ground before hacking away at him with their shovels, until all that remained was blood and gore. A fire was lit and his remains thrown on so that the vampire would be destroyed completely, never to return to harm their women.

The Berwick Vampire (2)

The second tale of Berwick's vampires I discovered when I paid a visit to the local library while researching *Supernatural North*. I was looking through some old files and books for potential ghost stories, when I read about an apparition that was also known as the Vampire of Berwick. Some suggest that this spectre was not a blood-sucking menace like the traditional vampire, but a pale, gaunt apparitional victim of the bubonic plague – one of the deadliest pandemics in human history, which first arrived in the 1300s and continued to devastate until the 1700s. Others, however, are not so sure!

This story is said to date back to the 1700s, when a very wealthy man died and was buried in the local churchyard. The 1856 English Historical Society's version of the *Historia Rerum Anglicarum* (a medieval sourcebook containing a concise history of England) is said to detail the story of this man, who rose from his grave after his death and terrorised the townsfolk of Berwick-upon-Tweed, accompanied by a howling pack of dogs. This walking corpse became known as the Vampire of Berwick and was feared by all who lived there. The people of the town were afraid to leave their houses at night for fear of running into the vampire, for it was said that the rotting stench of his decaying body could, and would, give those who smelt it an awful disease.

An image from 1864 of a vampire being killed in its grave by R. de Moraine. Did this really occur in Berwick back in the 1700s?

After being petrified for so long, the townsfolk of Berwick held a meeting and resolved to do something about this creature. It was decided that a group of young men would dig up the remains of the body, cut it into pieces, and then burn it to cinders. This they did and, at last, the spectre ceased to haunt the town, leaving the Berwick folk in peace to get on with their lives, safe in the knowledge they could rest easy at night.

There is, however, an eerie postscript to this tale. It is said that after the body of the vampire was burned and disposed of, one by one the group of men responsible slowly began to die horrible deaths. Some folk say it was the plague that they had caught from the corpse, but others suggest it was the dead vampire seeking his vengeance on the men.

The Berwick Vampire (3)

I discovered this narrative while leafing through the pages of one of the many books in my collection. *Haunted Britain*, by Elliott O'Donnell, is a well written tome that discusses many famous hauntings from across the UK. In his chapter 'Vampires and

Other North-Country Ghosts', he begins his opening paragraph with the sentence, 'It is very rarely one comes across an authentic record of vampires in England, and the following account of people who have wandered about after burial is probably unique.' He credits the account to William, Canon of Newburgh, who wrote the original version of the aforementioned *Historia Rerum Anglicarum*.

This is also where my second account of the Berwick vampire originates, so perhaps the two stories stem from the same tale, with subtle differences caused by years of telling. The following is Elliot O'Donnell's account from *Haunted Britain*:

> In Berwick on Tweed a certain citizen who appears to have amassed considerable wealth by anything but honest means, fell sick, died and was duly buried. Possibly owing to his evil reputation he had been excommunicated, and consequently was interred in unconsecrated ground. Be that as it may, we have Canon William's testimony for it that he came out of his grave night after night and haunted the countryside, pursued by a howling pack of ferocious phantom black dogs. People living in towns and villages were so fearful of the ghost that they barricaded themselves indoors, and even then were not safe, for he had all the vampire craving for human blood, and neither bolts nor bars were of any protection against his unwelcome visits.
>
> He used to bite and worry people to death, sucking the vitality out of them and not infrequently driving them mad; and owing to the foulness of his decayed body a pestilence arose which caused so many deaths that the higher and middle classes of the people held a necessary investigation into what was requisite to be done. As a result the body of the vampire was exhumed and burned, after which its ravages ceased.

The last two accounts are very similar indeed, though one places more emphasis on the 'vampire' being a plague-ridden apparition which haunted the town, and O'Donnell's narrative indicates an unholy, blood-sucking menace more akin to traditional vampires. Whatever the truth behind the vampire(s) of Berwick-upon-Tweed one thing is certain: they are spine-chilling tales to say the least. Are vampires just fictitious? Or are there really night-walking creatures that instil fear and dread into the heart of a community? William, Canon of Newburgh, clearly believed that the undead once walked in Berwick. Maybe he was right; and maybe they still do.

The Weeping Boy of Berwick's Quayside

It is thought that Berwick's most famous ghost is that of 'the weeping boy', a story said to date back to the mid-1700s involving a fisherman's young lad. Being the youngest child, the boy was not allowed to assist the family during their daily fishing trips out into the North Sea, and was – much to his dismay – made to stay at home. Every day his father and two older brothers ventured out in sometimes treacherous conditions to bring home their fresh supply of fish, and other types of seafood, for business purposes and for their own supply of fresh food. Day after day he would stay at home and worry himself silly about his family being out at sea, petrified that one day they would not return. Each day, however, they came back safe and sound and returned with an abundance of fresh seafood. One cold winter's day, the young boy was at home when suddenly he felt compelled to visit the quayside and await the return of his relations. What made him decide to do this no one knows, but some suggest that he sensed it was the last day he would ever see his family alive.

The youngster waited for hours in the ice-cold wind and rain and, as each minute ebbed slowly by, his gut instinct told him that something was wrong. Many hours passed and the family trawler in which they were fishing was long overdue. He felt a dreadful feeling in the pit of his stomach, which ultimately led the young lad to lose control of his emotions. He began to weep for his family as he knelt down at the docks facing the river mouth. The weeping soon became an uncontrollable bawl and it wasn't long before he was overheard by a passer-by. This kind soul ventured over to the young lad, and before she had a chance to ask what the matter was she too found herself crying and overcome with emotion. She pulled herself together and took the boy home to his mother. As it transpired, the boy's father and two brothers, whom he loved dearly, had died at sea and would never return.

Now the boy knew why he had never been allowed out to sea with the family. The ghost of the weeping boy can still be heard today and, by all accounts, has been seen on a number of occasions. Said to peer over the walls of Berwick and cry into the River Tweed, the ghost of this sad boy is supposed to either coincide with, or foretell, a death. The 'weeping boy' was even seen during the First World War. The sighting was around the time of the Battle of Mons on 23 and 24 August 1914, where nearly 7,000 people lost their lives.

The Battle of Mons, incidentally, lays claim to one of the most long-lived paranormal marvels that has ever been encountered. It is said that as the British and German armies were fighting on that fateful day in Belgium, a wondrous vision of a heavenly angel appeared and saved the British soldiers from what was ultimately going to be a vicious slaughtering. No one knows exactly how this protection occurred but some of the surviving soldiers later said a mysterious protective shield, or invisible force-field, somehow kept the enemy and their shells at bay. For many years now the 'Angel of Mons' has been seen by some as the ultimate divine intervention, though others suggest that the whole story was nothing more than mass hysteria and plain old wishful thinking.

The docks area of the town, where the ghost of the 'wailing boy' has been heard on many occasions.

The weeping boy of Berwick, it is said, was also seen on 22 November 1963, wandering around the docklands sobbing, with his head bowed. This was, eerily, hours before the assassination of the 35th President of the United States – John Fitzgerald Kennedy. In Dallas, Texas, at 12.30 p.m., he was shot once in the back and once in the head while riding in his Ford Lincoln car. Strangely, he is reported to have predicted his own death the day before he died, exclaiming, 'If somebody wants to shoot me from a window with a rifle, nobody can stop it, so why worry about it.'

One now wonders how many more times this ghost boy has been seen, and what deaths have coincided with his sighting?

It is thought that the world-famous escapologist Harry Houdini spent a lot of time and money researching the haunting of the weeping boy of Berwick, prior to his death in 1926. His findings have never been published.

The River Tweed and the Ghostly Galleon of the North Sea

The River Tweed spans approximately 97 miles from its source at Tweed's Well in the Lowther Hills near Moffat. It runs through the Tweed Valley and unites a number of major towns, primarily on the borders between England and Scotland, such as Tweedsmuir, Peebles, Selkirk, Galashiels, Melrose, Newstead, St Boswells, Kelso, and Coldstream before running through Berwick-upon-Tweed, where it flows into the North Sea. The river takes a very interesting course, with the first 75 miles or so being in Scotland. The next section of the Tweed sees the river itself becoming the border of England and Scotland, with the last section of the river being firmly in England. This is due to the fact that the last time Berwick was fought over, it was taken by the English.

The River Tweed is probably the last place anyone would think is haunted, but apparently it is. So what type of paranormal occurrences have been reported in the river? Could there be a spectral galleon or ghost ship silently sailing up the river before disappearing into the ether, leaving no trace of its existence? There is a distinct possibility that there could be spectral ships sailing the Tweed; after the Auld Alliance between France and Scotland had been agreed upon, there would have been many French battleships at the mouth of the Tweed, lying in wait, ready to attack the English port. To my knowledge, there have been no reports of this, although there have been sightings of ghostly galleons nearby, in the North Sea.

A few miles down the north-east coast, my friend and colleague Mike Hallowell was having a business meeting at a local inn (which just happens to be haunted too). Mike told me:

Over the North Sea, dark clouds billowed with the threat of rain, and we considered going back inside the inn. Slung around my neck was my camera, which, as a writer, I take everywhere with me. One never knows when an apparition may manifest itself and allow we earthbound mortals to capture it on celluloid. Such instances are rare, of course, but experience has taught me that, when ghost hunting, anything could happen. At some point I happened to gaze out to sea. The sky, grey and heavy-laden, merged imperceptibly with the ocean like one of Turner's paintings. Suddenly my eye caught an object bobbing up and down in the distance. As my eyes adjusted their focus I could see that it was a ship of some sort. This didn't surprise me as the mouth of the River Tyne lies to the north of the bay and a constant stream of vessels can be seen both entering and leaving on any given day. But there was something distinctly unusual about this ship; it was too tall. In my pocket I had a pair of opera glasses and by studying the ship through them I was able to make out more detail. To my astonishment I noticed that the vessel had both masts and sails.

Something – don't ask me what – told me that this was no ordinary vessel. My spine turned to ice and a strange sensation of 'otherworldliness' overtook me. For a brief moment the sun peeped out, and the delineation between sea and sky sharpened enormously. Fortunately I had the presence of mind to reach for my camera. I took three photographs of the ship. After the first shot I asked my wife and colleagues if they could see for themselves what I was looking at. At the same time the image of the ship started to change. Its outline became indistinct and blurry. The off-white colour of the sails faded distinctly and I knew that, whatever it was, it was about to fade from view. As I took the next two snaps, my wife and my two fellow journalists caught a fleeting glimpse of the vessel just before it faded into oblivion. To this day I do not know what I actually saw. It looked like a ship and rode the waves like a ship, and yet research determined that no sailing vessel of that nature left the River Tyne on that day. Was this a ghost ship from a previous century, sailing off to a destination now lost in the mists of time?

Heading back up north, we ask: what activity was reported in the Tweed? A cryptozoological creature like the famous Loch Ness Monster, or perhaps the ghost of someone drowning? No, the River Tweed is actually haunted by an occasional flow of blood! There are many ghost legends that feature the seeping or dripping

A most peculiar photograph of what is believed to be a ghost galleon taken on the horizon in the North Sea. This ship was said to slowly fade away into thin air in front of four people. (Photograph by Mike Hallowell)

blood of the dead, such as the irremovable bloodstains that blemish the floors and walls of certain haunted locations. Holyrood Palace in Edinburgh, for example, has a bloodstained floor in the Mary Queen of Scots room, and no matter how many times it is cleaned away it always seems to return. In the occasional poltergeist case, blood has been known to manifest itself in ways you would not believe. There is also the legend that Clifford's Tower in York drips with the blood of Jews who decided to kill themselves rather than be butchered by a violent mob in 1190.

Likewise, the River Tweed is said to run red with the phantom blood of the dead. During the Great Siege of 1296 that occurred during the reign of Edward I (*see* the section on Berwick Castle), the townsfolk were so horribly butchered that their blood flowed down the streets and into the river, whereupon it was washed downstream giving the whole river a red tinge. Perhaps this is not surprising, considering the brute force and vicious tactics that were employed in order to take the town. It is said that, on occasion, the River Tweed becomes flushed with the blood of those unfortunate townsfolk of Berwick who were so savagely murdered during Longshanks' campaign.

There are a number of tales that suggest the river of blood is not just a spooky legend that has been passed down through the generations. In Alan Robson's book *Grisly Trails and Ghostly Tales,* he recounts the grim story of a Newcastle lady who was visiting Berwick in the mid-1960s. Whilst there, she decided to meander along the riverbank. When she reached the 'low bridge' she allegedly saw the water begin to change colour from a grey-blue shade to a pinky-red colour. After a few minutes the river, according to Robson, was 'glimmering red'. Thinking her eyes were playing tricks on her, she decided not to dwell on it. After a while, though, she decided to enquire about what she saw and asked a local vicar. He subsequently explained the legend of Berwick's river of blood.

The River Tweed – said to have once flowed red with the blood of the dead.

Another tale Alan tells is the story of a young boy who was doing a bit of tiddler fishing during the 1970s. After putting his arm into the water for a few minutes, whilst holding on to a glass vessel (in the hope of scooping up some small fish), he lifted his arm out the river to find the jar full of cloudy dark red water. Certainly not what he was expecting to see! After throwing it away and trying again a little further down the river, he found that the water was clear again.

The Brewers Arms Pub

There are not many haunted pubs in Berwick. I have paced the streets from one end of the town to the other in search of them, mostly to no avail. An exception to this is the Brewers Arms – and a couple more pubs that I discovered by chance on the other side of the Tweed in the Spittal area.

The Brewers Arms is situated in the centre of Castlegate on Berwick's main high street and is reputed to house a ghost or two. I called in for a pint during my excursions round town in 2008 to see if I could glean any information regarding the ghosts. A friendly barmaid told me that she had heard the pub was haunted, but couldn't tell me who or what haunted it. I then asked her colleague, who informed me that strange occurrences had been witnessed from time to time in the pub.

Apparently, the activity became so bothersome at one time that a team of paranormal investigators was asked to visit the pub and carry out some tests. I managed to find out who this team was and contacted one of their members, a woman called Sue. I was told by Sue that although some peculiar occurrences were documented on the night of their overnight investigation, they were largely subjective and left the team with very little to go on. I then tried to find out exactly what had been happening at this pub; the information I received from the bar staff was that objects quite often flew off the shelves and a presence had been felt in various parts of the premises. During my most recent trip to Berwick, in autumn 2009, I found that the paranormal experiences at the pub had subsided to the point of non-existence.

The Queens Head Hotel

Located in Sandgate, at the bottom of Hide Hill, stands the Queens Head Hotel. This is a wonderful old hotel-cum-restaurant that dates back many years. I couldn't resist popping in for a quick chat with the staff to see if they had experienced any strange activity at the hotel. As I ventured in through the front doors I was struck

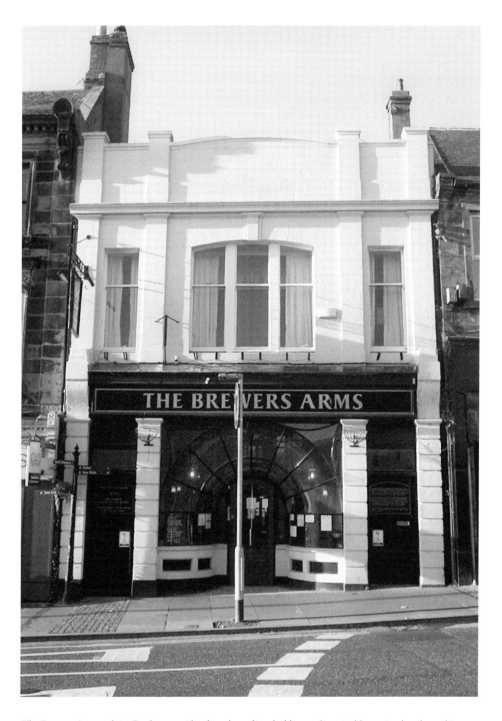

The Brewers Arms pub in Castlegate, said to have been disturbed by a poltergeist-like entity that threw things around and tinkered with the bar fittings.

by the hotel's immaculate appearance. Everything was pristine and in its place. Not a speck of dust lay anywhere in the building – or so it seemed – and the staff inside the premises were smartly dressed. I was impressed.

As I walked through the entrance lobby, I was greeted by a good-looking young lady on the reception desk. I asked her if the establishment had any ghosts and was told that she had no idea. 'I suppose there may be, considering the building is so old,' she said.

Just then, another member of staff popped her head around the corner and greeted me. The receptionist explained to her that I was looking for ghosts and asked if she knew about any spirits the hotel may have. This lady then explained that Room 3 of the hotel had 'strange things about it'. When I asked her what she meant she said she thought that odd things had occurred there in times gone by.

The Queen's Head Hotel. Room 3 allegedly has 'strange things about it'.

This information was not elaborated on. However, in my quest to unearth tales of spectres and shades, the receptionist told me a very interesting story about a haunted house on nearby Church Street – the street where I happened to be staying that night. She told me this with total conviction, as the haunted house on Church Street was her family home when she was a child.

A Haunting on Church Street

Church Street is a relatively quiet street in Berwick with a number of private residences and an abundance of hotels and bed & breakfasts that stretch all the way up to the top of the road. The Berwick Barracks are at the top of Church Street (along the Parade), and where Church Road joins with Wallace Green you will see the gates to the great ramparts of Berwick. Here you will see the great Cumberland Bastion standing before you.

During my research, I stayed at a beautifully-run bed & breakfast called Ben More House, which is situated at No. 51 Church Street. The hospitality I received from the owner, Lynne Ellerby, was exemplary and the building itself is a Grade II listed Georgian townhouse that oozes charm and character. Not far away stands another building, with a very different type of character.

I will not specify which house it is, as somebody could be living there today in blissful ignorance of the house's former reputation. At one time sinister things occurred at this house on Church Street, which left a family scratching their heads in disbelief and convinced that they had been visited by someone, or something, from the other side.

The receptionist at the Queens Head Hotel told me that, as a child, she and her family would often find various household objects moved from their original position and left elsewhere, where they should not have been. Temperature drops were also noted, and some of the rooms would suddenly become ice-cold. She said that 'strange sensations' were felt in the house and, when I asked her what she meant, she couldn't quite put her finger on it. 'I guess it was like feeling that someone was there with you when you know there wasn't. Does that make sense?'

'Perfectly,' I replied. 'What else occurred in the house?'

'Well, getting the feeling of being watched occurred quite a lot, and I did not like that one bit,' she said. 'My parents also felt as though invisible eyes looked down on them when they were going about their everyday household duties.'

She went on to tell me that these odd happenings went on for a few years, until eventually they moved out of the house. It was not the alleged ghost that chased the family out, though, but circumstances in regards to work. She told me that she

Church Street, Berwick. One of these houses was once subjected to a whole host of paranormal activity when the receptionist of the Queen's Head Hotel lived there.

had never been so glad to leave a house behind and since then she and her family have had no trouble with ghosts or the unexplained. In fact, she told me that when I came into the hotel to enquire about ghosts, it had brought it all back.

I remember the look on her face when she suddenly recalled the strange incidents she had experienced while growing up, and she seemed genuine. I have become experienced at spotting when someone is feeding me a line and I got the impression that this lady was telling the truth. The next story is another great example of what I would consider to be a bona-fide account from a bona-fide gentleman.

The Kings Mount Redcoat

It's amazing what you can find out when you ask around. When I visited The Barrels public house on Bridge Street to ask about ghosts, I was told that no ghosts resided at the pub: 'Well, at least if there is, we have never come across them.' Sitting in the corner was an old gentleman getting stuck-in to his pint of bitter and reading a newspaper. He had a long coat on, flat cap and glasses, and looked to be between seventy-five and eighty years of age. As I was about to leave the pub – in dismay – a voice came booming across the room.

'You want to hear ghost stories do you?'

'I do indeed. Have you got one to tell?' I asked him.

'Yes, but I have to leave in twenty, so if you want it, we'd better be quick,' said the man.

I sat down next to him, turned my tape recorder on, and began to listen intently to what he had to say.

'What is your interest in ghosts then lad?' he asked, as he took a mouth of ale. I told him that I was researching a book on the ghost tales of Berwick and was in the area to unearth new stories that could feature within the volume.

'It's your lucky day then lad,' he said.

'I have a tale to acquaint you with that I have not told in almost thirty years, and it is about a very queer happening that occurred to me back in the late 1970s.'

This harrowing account occurred within throwing distance of Coxon's Tower. If you follow the path up towards the ramparts in the south-east area of the town, you will come to Kings Mount. As you walk steadily up the incline and along the pathway at the top you will eventually come to the Windmill Bastion. It is between these two points that the ghost of a Redcoat was seen, twice! The elderly gent continued:

I was out walking my dog early one winter's morning – like I always did – and nothing seemed out of the ordinary. It was dawn, freezing cold, and I was looking forward to returning home to a nice pot of tea. When I approached the steep hill that leads up to Windmill Bastion, I decided – for some unknown reason – to take a different route. Usually I would have gone down onto the lane, through the arched bridge, and along the seafront towards the pier and lighthouse. This time I walked straight on and, after putting the dog on his lead, I began to tackle the sharp hill that leads to the top of the ramparts. I wish I hadn't.

Upon getting to the top of the hill's brow, I turned around to admire the early morning view across the river and there on the path, halfway up the hill (about 50ft away), was a man holding a long stick. He stood ever so still and he seemed to be staring at me. I turned for a brief second to tend to the dog, and when I turned back around he was gone. I thought nothing of this and continued my stroll. After ten minutes or so I approached the Windmill Bastion section of the ramparts, when suddenly I became rooted to the spot with abject fear and I didn't know why. I plucked up the courage to turn around, as I felt there was somebody behind me, and there – this time no more than 10ft away from where I stood – was the same man that I had seen earlier. This time, as it was a little lighter, I could determine that the fellow was wearing an old soldier's costume and the stick I thought he was carrying earlier was in fact a gun with a sword on the end.

I asked if he could describe the man he saw that morning.

I will never forget him. He had red pants that were tucked into long white socks, and a strange red jacket that stopped at his thighs. Across his body, from one shoulder to the waist, was a white or grey stripe and on his back I could see some sort of carrier, or a bag. The oddest thing about this guy was that he had on a three-cornered hat, like a highwayman wears. He also had what looked like a sword down by his side.

'So what did you do?' I asked him.
'I ran like hell,' came the reply. Then he added:

There was something just not right about him. The first time I saw him I knew there was something untoward about his presence, an eerie feel, even sinister. So when I saw him again standing 10ft away, just staring at me, I lost it and ran. It was a ghost alright; mark my words.

The old gentleman doesn't venture that way any more as the whole experience has left him quite traumatised.

I switched off my dictation machine, drank up my beer, and thanked this kind gentleman because, after thirty years, he had decided to share his story with me, and, with his permission, I now share with you.

Following this account I couldn't resist doing some research and was astonished to find out that, during the mid-1740s, a troop of soldiers known as the English Redcoats was based at Berwick as this town was one of their key garrisons. In fact, there is some information on the ramparts opposite the Berwick Barracks explaining this. The thought occurs that the story could have been a wind-up, but my gut instinct tells me it was not. However, it is not impossible, which leaves two possibilities: a) I was reeled in hook, line and sinker, or b) the section of the ramparts between Kings Mount and Windmill Bastion is haunted by a Redcoat soldier.

If the story is a true account, as I suspect it is, then perhaps the ghost has been seen on other occasions. If there is anyone out there who can shed some light on this story, I would love to hear about it.

The lonely stretch of path on King's Mount near Windmill Bastion, where the ghost of an English Redcoat was seen by a man walking his dog in the 1970s.

An artist's impression of the English Redcoat Soldier ghost. (Picture by Julie Olley)

Berwick Barracks, seen from nearby Kings Mount and close to where the ghostly Redcoat was seen.

The Gate House, Sandgate

While looking for ghosts in the neighbouring Hen and Chickens Hotel at Sandgate (there were none) I was told about an alleged ghost that once resided in the now disused gate house that stands opposite. A chap at the hotel claimed that he knew somebody who had lived at the gate house many years ago who, in turn, claimed that some odd occurrences had happened there. The building (at the time of writing) stands empty and derelict, which is a great shame.

The chap informed me that there have been reports of a mystery woman peering out of the windows in the attic space of the building. These windows are high up but can be clearly seen from the walkway that stretches along the Berwick Walls, over the Sandgate entrance to the town.

After hearing the tale, I decided to venture up the stairs to the house and knock on the door; I got no answer. I peered inside the windows and could clearly see that no one was actually living there.

The area of Sandgate was once dominated by tradesmen known as the salmon coopers, who put together the equipment for exporting fish to places such as

London. The salmon trade on the River Tweed was so significant in those days that the coopers eventually came to rule shipping and commerce within Berwick. I was told that 'a tall tower on the right' (could this be the gate house?) was part of the former corn exchange which was built in 1858 as a market for corn merchants.

Interestingly, I also found out via some serious snooping that a woman in Victorian attire has been seen climbing the stairwell leading up to the top of the Berwick Walls – right next to the gate house. She begins her ascent next to the cobbled road, but she never actually reaches the top of the stairs! She seems to disappear about halfway up. Another woman fitting this description has been seen under the actual arch, along the cobblestones in the direction of Sandgate. One wonders if these women, and the one who has been seen looking out from a window of the gate house, are one and the same?

The archway in the wall near the Gate House, where a woman in Victorian attire has been seen walking along the cobblestones in the direction of Sandgate.

The Gate House on Sandgate.

St Aidan's House

St Aidan's House on Palace Green is reputed to be haunted. I was told that the building (which stands unused at the time of writing) is haunted by 'strange footfalls, creaky floorboards and flitting shadows'. I could find out little about this building as every time I have gone to explore it, it has been locked up and access has been rather difficult. On searching for the building online I also came up with nothing.

However, through a conversation I had with a couple of local folk I learned that the building has a ghost. A couple of passers-by, who happened to notice me when I was knocking on the door, voiced the opinion that I would 'have a job getting in there'. They told me that they lived locally and thought (or at least had heard rumours) that the building was 'spooked out'.

They said that many years ago the building had gained the reputation of having a ghost. All they knew for sure was that strange things had happened to former cleaning staff and personnel who used the building. Whether or not St Aidan's House is really haunted is hard to say, especially if the alleged ghosts are based solely on anecdotal stories and hearsay. However, the building itself does have a distinctly haunting look about it and it wouldn't surprise me if there was something in it. For the time being we can only speculate.

Palace Green in Berwick, c. 1925. The tank is from the First World War and the building in the background is St Aidan's House. (Courtesy of Newcastle Libraries and Information Service)

A splendid view – taken from the top of the spire at the Town Hall – of the rooftops of Berwick and Spittal in the distance, c. 1930. (Courtesy of Newcastle Libraries and Information Service)

Kwik Save

All I know of this site is that it was the scene of a frightening encounter before the premises was converted into a supermarket. I was informed during one of my many trips to Berwick, by numerous locals, that something occurred in the premises which left its mark on a few people.

'You should try asking at the old Kwik Save, there was a ghost in there,' I was told.

This is a request from the author to have the full story relayed to him by someone who may know it in its entirety. If you know what happened there, or who the ghost of Kwik Save is, please get in touch and let me know.

Berwick Bridge and the River Tweed.

two

Berwickshire Ghosts (Hauntings on the Outskirts)

The Blenheim Hotel's Ghost That Never Was, Spittal, Berwick-upon-Tweed

It can be rather accidental how ghosts or haunted locations are discovered. During an amble around Berwick, in search of haunted locations, I ventured into one inn where I was told about a terrifying ghost that resided in another pub on

The Blenheim Hotel – no ghosts, but a fantastic pint of Blenheim Bitter!

the other side of the water. I was informed that a horrific murder took place many years ago. The victim, a girl said to be in her early teens, allegedly haunts the pub because that was where she once lived. I was told that her former bedroom, above the inn, was permanently freezing cold due to her presence. When I asked where this pub – the Blenheim Hotel – was, I was informed it was in Spittal, and a bus would be required for me to get there.

As it transpired, the pub did not have any spirits residing there – unless you count the Jack Daniels, the vodka, and the whisky bottles hanging upside-down over the bar!

I walked almost two miles to find out that the Blenheim Hotel was not haunted. However, had I not ventured across to Spittal to find this lovely old alehouse, I would never have discovered two other ghost tales that are rather well known in these parts – it's a funny old world.

The Red Lion Inn, Spittal, Berwick-upon-Tweed

The Red Lion public house is a typical local boozer, where clientele play dominoes almost all afternoon and *Grandstand* is shown on the television mounted on the wall. I love this type of pub. The Red Lion dates back to around 1821 and I was told that it could well have been another pub before that. As I was walking past – on my way to the aforementioned Blenheim Hotel – I saw two gentlemen standing outside, enjoying roll-up cigarettes. I approached these gentlemen after one said 'Good afternoon' and asked them if the Red Lion had any ghosts.

To my delight I was told that the pub was indeed haunted, a fact that was quite well known by the locals. I asked who I should speak to about the ghosts of the Red Lion and was promptly informed that I should speak to the manager, Paul Angus.

I ventured into the pub and saw a middle-aged fellow behind the bar serving the locals their beers. This was Paul. The two chaps who had been smoking their roll-ups followed me in and quite loudly introduced me by saying, 'Paul, this lad here wants to hear the ghost stories.' We said hello, and after he finished serving a few more beers, he came across and spoke to me.

'I remember many years ago there was a book written about seaside villages and places to stay and Spittal was in it,' he said. 'The Red Lion was in the book too, along with its spooky reputation.'

I asked him what sort of ghostly phenomena had been experienced in the pub.

We used to have people stay over here, in rooms, like a hotel, and one Friday night a few years ago we had some guests coming in. We have one big bedroom upstairs that has four beds in, so my wife went into the room to prepare it for our guests. After a while I went upstairs to see where my wife was and yelled out, 'Are you done yet?' to which she replied, 'Yes, I have finished the beds'. I looked into the room and saw one bed in the corner that had not been made up and said to the missus, 'What about this bed?' She yelled back that she had made them all. When she came back into the main bedroom, she was astonished to see that the blankets had been pulled out and were strewn everywhere, as though the bed had just been slept in. Furthermore, there was now an indent on the mattress, as though someone was sitting down on the bed. It was really strange.

I then asked Paul if anything else had occurred that he would put down to paranormal activity. He answered in the affirmative:

I lost my wedding ring once, not this one [he points towards a new wedding ring] but an older one that I had. I lost it for about five years. Then, one morning, when I was getting out of bed, I stepped on it. There it was; it appeared out of the blue. How many times had I hoovered that floor, stepped out of that bed? I would have seen it for sure if it was there, and it sure wasn't there the night before when I went to bed. It's puzzling.

Other things have been experienced at the bar too, with the clinking of glasses being heard while no one was in the bar – as though an invisible glass collector was at work. Taps have also been interfered with on the pumps that are kept down in the cellars. 'Many a time I come to pull a pint and find the taps have been turned off,' Paul said.

I explained to Paul that all of these incidents were the typical activity of a mischievous ghost (perhaps even a poltergeist). Paul then told me one more chilling tale:

Over the road [points to a house out the pub window] there used to be a fella who was a head smuggler to some organised group that once worked the area around Spittal. Everyone knew of his crimes and they became fed up of the riches he had due to his line of work, while everyone else lived with almost nothing and had to work damn hard for it. Well, behind the Red Lion pub there was once a blacksmith's workshop and it was in there where the locals decided to mete out some of their own justice. The locals had a word with the blacksmith and it was decided that they would shackle him up in chains, gag him, and leave him to die.

And that, according to Paul, is what they did. Nothing was heard from the chained-up smuggler except the odd whimper, as he tried in vain to free himself. It took about a week for him to slowly slip away into the next world.

The Red Lion pub in Spittal, haunted by a ghost that likes to mess up beds, and a smuggler of old – his chains clinking as he makes his way down the old alley behind the pub at midnight.

An artist's impression of the ghost of the murdered smuggler making his way down the old alley behind the Red Lion pub in Spittal. (Picture by Julie Olley)

It is said that if you listen out at around midnight, you can hear the rattle and clinking of the spectral smuggler bound in his chains, making his way down the alley behind the Red Lion, as he desperately seeks some assistance. The thought occurs that the ghost of this smuggler may also be the resident spectre of the Red Lion pub. I dare say he would have frequented the alehouse when he was alive, and with the pub being the focal point of the village, perhaps his downfall was planned by the locals there. Haunting the Red Lion could be his way of telling the villagers that they will never be rid of him.

The Galleon Pub, Spittal, Berwick-upon-Tweed

Before I left the Red Lion alehouse, I was informed of another pub that was even more frightening. Paul Angus told me that, a few doors down, there once stood a

The house in Spittal which was once a pub known as The Galleon. The pub closed for business back in 2003/4 after poltergeist activity terrorised the landlord, his family and the locals. The haunting made the national newspapers in 1991, but since its closure the ghost has been seen no more.

drinking den with a reputation for being horribly haunted – to the point where no tenant would stay there for fear of harm coming to them. The pub was called the Galleon. Paul told me:

> Big strapping men would be sitting having their lunch, and after they had paid a visit to the loos they would just get their families and run. Something in there terrified them, and that happened on a regular basis. The pub was even exorcised by the head priest of Hexham. Things really got that bad and it was known to be the most haunted pub in and around Berwick. The pub is now somebody's house. Can you believe that? You should find out about that one.

Upon leaving the Red Lion, I meandered down the street to see if I could find the building which was formerly the Galleon. It didn't take me long to find, as there were small clues that gave its location away; I saw a building with small holes in the wall which indicated a sign had once hung outside. My assumption was confirmed by one of the locals, Eddie MacDonald, who told me that he lived next door to the former pub. His wife, Sheila, had been a barmaid in the Galleon many years ago. I had struck gold.

Eddie went into his house and called for his wife. I asked her if she thought the former pub was haunted and she replied, 'Oh yes.' She was quite happy to tell me the ghost stories surrounding the place. She explained that although they had experienced nothing in their own house, she had experienced odd things while working at the Galleon. Glasses would be thrown about by invisible hands, ice-cold breezes would 'rush' through the place despite all the windows being closed, and something 'otherworldly' resided in the back passageway near the gents loos that would scare the hell out of folks paying a visit. I was then informed that the haunting made headlines in the newspapers after a former landlord was attacked by the spirit in the cellar. The entity apparently disliked the landlord and tried to dispatch him by hurling a full beer barrel, weighing almost a ton, at him! It just missed him, but gave him the stark warning that it wanted him out.

Before this building (somewhere on Main Street) was a pub, I was told that it was a local bakery and it too had the reputation of being haunted. An old woman who worked at the bakery died one day, and her spirit simply refused to leave. Many a time she was seen in the old shop behind the counter and around the store in general, and although Sheila admits she never saw this ghostly lady, she knows plenty of people who did.

Eddie had left while I was speaking to his wife and when he reappeared he was holding a newspaper clipping from 1991 which told the story of the haunting and the subsequent attempted exorcism. 'Demon Hurled Barrel at Me', read the headline, and the article told how the eighty-eight pint barrel was thrown across the room and smashed into a doorframe. It also explained that the 'demon' showed itself to people in the back passageway, and sometimes in the bar area. The spirit would call out the landlord's wife's name and turn off the taps. Drinkers would often flee from the pub after experiencing odd phenomena and, after losing over four stone due to stress, the landlord had the place exorcised. Since then, the landlord believed that the 'demon' was gone and there were no more abnormal incidents in the pub thereafter.

It must be stressed that the site of this former pub (which opened in 1978 and closed for business in 2003/4) is now a private house and no attempt must be made to go 'ghost hunting'. Respect must be given to the property, its owners and the locals alike. Please bear in mind that the haunting ceased in 1991 after the exorcism, and no further paranormal occurrences have been witnessed since that time.

A Haunted House in Scremerston, Berwickshire

Ghosts, for those who are unaware of their lore, don't just reside in large stately homes situated in the centre of 100-acre parks. Nor are they confined to ancient castles – ruined or otherwise – pubs, clubs, old prisons, towers and such like.

Ghosts find accommodation in the most unusual of places, so if you thought you were safe in your own humble abode, think again. In fact, there are many documented cases of 'two up, two down' houses being haunted. A young couple in Scremerston near Berwick – who shall remain anonymous – know this only too well, after experiencing some odd paranormal activity which began in their home in the late 1990s.

Having investigated the now infamous 'South Shields Poltergeist' case back in 2006, I can say with conviction that strange occurrences can and do find their way into everyday homes and terrorise the householders to the point of nervous breakdown. Of course, cases like the one in South Shields are very rare indeed, and the house in Scremerston experienced little by comparison. However, the Scremerston couple undeniably suffered frightening experiences in their home, and consequently called in a colleague of mine to help them and document the activity. In fact the haunting, as it turned out, was something of an unorthodox case which turned out to have a surprising conclusion.

The trouble began around 1999, not long after the couple moved into the house. Whispering voices were heard by the occupants when no one else was in the property and, every now and again, a strange bump or bang would be heard but nothing was ever thought of it. This occurred for a few years and the couple put up with it, not knowing for sure if the noises they were hearing were normal, or paranormal. Eventually, the couple realised that they had a ghost when they both saw a male figure – at the same time – standing on the landing area of the house. The gentleman of the house was standing in one room at the time of the sighting and the lady in another room entirely. This is quite interesting – one ghostly figure that was observed from two different view points. Sightings do not normally occur like this as spirits are usually viewed from one angle, even when there is more than one witness.

The lady of the house was initially unnerved by what was happening in her home but eventually she became rather intrigued by it. This is quite often the case in situations like this, with people eventually becoming either interested or bored, as opposed to being frightened. The gentleman, on the other hand, had a lot of trouble accepting the fact that his house was haunted.

Eventually, after becoming tired of the strange occurrences, the couple decided to enlist the help of a Northumbrian-based researcher, Suzanne Hitchinson (*née* McKay). Suzanne, from Warkworth, Northumberland, is a member of the North East Ghost Research Team, which the author founded in 2003. Being on the team, Suzanne was fortunate enough to have experienced some of the bewildering phenomena that occurred during the South Shields case. She is pretty clued up in matters concerning the paranormal world and the couple at Scremerston made a good choice when they contacted her. I spoke to Suzanne about the investigation she ran at the house and this is what she had to say:

> I was invited up to investigate the house at Scremerston in 2007. The occupants of the house had been experiencing unnerving, unexplained noises, with the female of the house frequently seeing shadows. On a more sinister level, she claimed to see ghostly faces in the mirrors. Her husband had also witnessed some of the activity and they wanted some answers on what could have been causing the problem.
>
> On interviewing the couple I discovered that a certain member of her family had sadly died in a tragic accident and at a very young age, and she told us that, on occasion, the face in the mirror was her deceased relative.
>
> During an overnight investigation we held there, nothing was recorded on our video cameras, nor were any strange recordings made. The EMF sweep, which shows the readings within the electro-magnetic fields, showed no anomalous results either.
>
> Being psychic, I decided to see what I could pick up on – if anything. I soon picked up on two individual spirits that occasionally visited, but essentially meant no harm. I identified a young male and an older female presence, both believed to be relatives of the adult female of the house. The spirits who stepped forward on that night passed on a few private messages to the couple, and for obvious reasons they will remain private.
>
> No residual energies were picked up on on the night, and the team that had visited found no conclusive, objective evidence to deem the residence haunted.
>
> My team still have frequent contact with the couple in Scremerston, and they have told me that since we visited the house it does seem a bit calmer, though they sometimes still have strange things occur. However, I think that they can now rest easy in the knowledge that these spirits are not permanent at their home, rather a family member or two merely popping in to say 'hi' in whatever way they can.

An interesting story, illustrating the fact that not all ghosts are intent on causing misery to those with whom they share a dwelling.

Pearlin Jean and the Haunting of Allanbank, Berwickshire

I wonder how many of the good folk of Berwickshire today are aware of a house, known to be the home of a tragic tale of love, betrayal and tragedy, that once stood in their picturesque county. Elliot O'Donnell, in his book *Scottish Ghost Stories*, says that, 'Few ghosts have obtained more notoriety than Pearlin Jean, the phantasm which for many years haunted Allanbank, a seat of the Stuarts.'

Allanbank House is unfortunately now long gone, as it was destroyed in the early nineteenth century, but the ghost that was said to reside there is still well-remembered by the serious psychical researcher. Written up in a number of tomes, the story of Pearlin Jean was one of Berwickshire's more famous ghost legends, but potentially one of the least known today.

Why, I wondered, was the ghost of this one-time abode named Pearlin Jean? I presumed that Jean was the name of the lady in question, and I was correct. But Pearlin? Well, that turned out to be the distinct pattern of lace that was worn on her favourite dress and collar. I guess it is like naming a ghost the 'Grey Lady' simply because she is wearing a grey dress, or calling ghost women 'silkies' if they wear silk dresses.

Jean is said to have been the lover of Robert Stuart, the first Baronet of Allanbank, and she loved him dearly. Jean, in some accounts, is also said to have been a French nun who gave up her life in Paris to come to Berwickshire and be with her true-love after their liaisons had begun. The couple loved each other for a while – until Robert decided that Jean was not good enough to be his wife. He began to court another young lady and eventually married her. Jean, in the meantime, was left abandoned and alone in a country she knew little about, with people she did not know. She had given up everything to be with Robert, burning all her metaphorical bridges when she left – therefore returning home was simply not an option.

There was only one thing for it; she decided to try and win her lover back. But how was this to be done? He was now a happy newly-wed, but she felt that she had to try. One day, Robert was leaving his house – Allanbank – in his horse-drawn carriage when out from nowhere came Jean. She must have been hiding in the roadside foliage awaiting his journey. Jean allegedly jumped desperately onto the speeding carriage as it thundered past, with the sole intention of speaking to Robert. She hoped, in vain, that he would see the error of his ways and take her back. That was her plan but, like most good ghost stories, it ended in tragedy.

There are two accounts of how Robert reacted after Jean leapt onto the coach. The first suggests that he got a bit of a fright; the other suggests that he was horrified, as he had not seen her for some time and didn't want to either. Regardless of how he felt when he was confronted by his former lover, his response was immediate. After casting his eyes on her clinging to the side of the carriage, he suddenly whipped the horses into a frenzy, jolting the entire carriage as he did so. This resulted in poor Jean losing her grip and being thrown from the side of the carriage. As she fell, her long dress was caught in the carriage wheels and she was dragged under the passenger coach. She was inevitably crushed to death by the huge and heavy-duty wheels. Robert felt the carriage rise up and then come back down as he rode over his former lover. Her neck was broken, her backbone severed and her head was almost torn off – spurting warm blood all over the underside of the carriage.

In some accounts of this tale, Robert is said to have been distraught at what he had done and was horrified to see the mangled corpse of Jean under his wheels. Other versions suggest that he thought nothing of it, and after crushing her to death he continued his journey as though nothing had occurred. The vision of the accident, however, is said to have preoccupied him for some time to come (as it would anyone), but it was not just the memory of that fateful day that came back to haunt him; the ghost of Jean did too.

The first sighting of Jean was observed by Robert on his return home to Allanbank after being away on business. As he approached the gates to the house, he was dumbfounded to see a white figure that seemed to be glowing slightly. As he got closer he realised that the head of this white apparition was covered in blood! The ghost woman stared at Robert with a hatred in her eyes which sent shivers down his spine. He was horrified at the vision of Pearlin Jean and was rendered speechless with absolute fear.

For many years after Jean's death, her restless and angry spirit is said to have caused mayhem and upset at Allanbank House. Doors inside the house would often be slammed hard when no one was near them, and her ghost was seen there on a number of occasions. She haunted Robert Stuart to his dying day. Even after his death, the ghost of Pearlin Jean was seen and experienced at Allanbank. New tenants of the house were perfectly aware of the ghost – who by this time had calmed down in regards to her frightening activities – and regarded her as something of a fixture and fitting of the property, and even felt some affection for her. Visitors to the house, however, who were not aware of the tragic tale or her spectre, were often startled by her sudden appearances and her mischievous tricks.

One tale tells of a courting couple who had made secret plans to meet up in the orchard of Allanbank garden. The young man, Thomas, had made his way to meet his lover, Jenny, and arrived at their designated meeting point thirty minutes early. While he stood there, in amongst the moonlit trees, the figure of a lady in white appeared whom he mistook for Jenny. Thomas rushed towards her, greeting her with a hug – only to discover that when he hugged her she completely vanished.

He then fled into the night, terrified, leaving the real Jenny to turn up at the correct time and be met by no one. After waiting for her beloved for a short while, Jenny returned to the great house. The following morning, all was explained to the bewildered Jenny. She duly forgave Thomas and eventually the couple were married.

In another tale, two women were permitted to stay at Allanbank House. They had no idea that the house was haunted until they experienced the phenomenon for themselves during the course of their stay. Sleeping in the same bedroom, they were simultaneously disturbed from their slumbers by the sound of someone pacing heavily across their bedroom floor. The footsteps were accompanied by the swishing of a garment and the sound of breathing, but as it was dark they couldn't see who, or what, was there. Frozen to their beds with fear, all they could do was hope and pray that the spectral intruder would not come any closer to them. They were too frightened to move or get up, so they stayed petrified in their beds until the ghost went away. They had a long wait, as the ghost did not stop pacing back and forth until the room was lit by the morning sun. After this harrowing episode, they were informed by the house owner of the tale of Pearlin Jean.

The house at Allanbank was demolished many years ago, and it seems that when the house disappeared, so did the ghost of Pearlin Jean. No more accounts came in of a bloodied ghost in white with gruesome head injuries, and the mischievous activity and slamming doors ceased. Perhaps Jean was able to rest in peace after the house was finally demolished, putting an end to her suffering. Her ghost is now long gone, but I am sure her tragic tale will be remembered for many years to come.

The Victorian Girl of Haggerston Castle, Berwickshire

'Ghost Busters Called As Berwick Holiday Park Staff Get The Creeps' was the headline in one of the north-east's best-known newspapers a few years ago, after strange occurrences were experienced by staff at the tourist attraction.

There were regular sightings of a young Victorian girl inside the building known as the Rotunda, a building with a circular ground plan which dominated the holiday park. This girl has also been observed in the cellar of the building, accompanied by eerie, unexplained noises.

One employee of the park, while working alone in this particular Grade II listed building, experienced some odd activity. He said that the temperature suddenly plummeted for no apparent reason and then the radio in the room came on. The radio buzzed quite loudly and so the staff member thought it was the ghost wanting

The tower at Haggerston Castle near Berwick.
(Photograph taken by Teresa Burn)

An artist's impression of the Victorian girl reported
to have been seen in the cellars of the Rotunda at
Haggerston Castle. (Picture by Julie Olley)

'to play'. On another occasion, a heavy music system was mysteriously moved from a shelf in an empty room and placed on the floor.

A team of paranormal enthusiasts from Falkirk went to investigate the hauntings, and experienced some rather interesting things. This, however, was not the first time ghost hunters had investigated the building. On another occasion, a different paranormal team heard footsteps in a room upstairs, while they themselves were downstairs in the ancient tower. The sound of metal being dragged across one of the tower's floors has also been heard.

It is interesting to note that the grounds in which Haggerston Castle stands were apparently cursed by a local witch when a previous estate occupied the area hundreds of years ago. Following this curse there is said to have been three fires on the site. The first fire is thought to have occurred when the former estate was in its prime. The second and third fires were in the 1600s and early 1900s. No one knows why this alleged curse was placed upon the land but it is thought – and hoped – that the curse has now been fulfilled.

Afterword

What an absolute joy it has been to pen this, the very first book on the ghosts and spooky tales of Berwick-upon-Tweed and Berwickshire. That said, it has been very hard work. At times I thought I would never meet my publisher's target for the final word count, but through sheer tenacity and my endless determination to seek out the ghosts of this small, historical town, I have prevailed. Achieving this required many trips to Berwick and some serious ghost hunting. After pacing the ancient streets from dawn till dusk, and calling in at just about every place I could think of, I sought out the stories this town had to offer.

Ghost hunting is not about spending one single night in a haunted location, with highly modern gadgetry such as K2 EMF meters and night-vision video recorders, hoping and praying that you will see a phantom. Granted, this is rewarding to a certain extent – I have done hundreds of these overnight vigils, with some quite surprising results. Out of all these overnight investigations, however, I have only ever seen one ghost. I have witnessed an abundance of other types of paranormal phenomena over the years, including being pushed over by invisible hands, recording and hearing ghostly footfalls, seeing doors slammed shut, and experiencing furniture being turned over when no one was near it. If you go looking for it, and you are honest in your reporting, you will eventually see genuine paranormal activity for yourself.

But you don't have to spend nights waiting in haunted places to learn stories of ghosts. My previous books, *Haunted Newcastle* and *Haunted Durham*, consist of many tales of the supernatural that I have personally discovered simply by making impromptu visits to random pubs and other buildings within these cities. On one

An 1890s view of Old Berwick Bridge taken from Tweedmouth. (Courtesy of Newcastle Libraries and Information Service)

The old stocks, standing as a reminder of days of old, are located near the stone stairs leading to the Town Hall.

occasion, while researching the ghosts of York, I booked myself into the most haunted pub in the city – the Golden Fleece – for one night, on my own, to see if anything would occur. I took very little in the way of equipment and had no desire to sit up all night partaking in vigils. I simply turned in at around midnight and went to sleep. I was not disturbed during my slumbers by spectres standing over my bed, I heard no footfalls or anything of that nature while lying in the darkness, nor did I experience the bed shaking while I was lying in it (one of the many reputed phenomena that have been reported in the Minster Suite). Nothing occurred this time, but the point is that anybody can try this type of ghost hunting.

In Berwick, I got to chat with many wonderful people, saw some weird and wonderful places within the locations featured herein, but most of all I discovered a plethora of new tales of hauntings and ghost lore that I had hitherto not heard of.

Berwick-upon-Tweed, with its ancient walls, side streets and back lanes, is an historical place. Wherever you may roam, keep your eyes open and your ears to the ground, for you may just run into one of the many echoes or shades of the past that inhabit this little northern town close to the Scottish border.

Bibliography & Sources

Day, James Wentworth, *In Search of Ghosts* (Muller, 1969)

Dodds, Derek, *Northumbria at War* (Pen & Sword, 2005)

Fuller, Dr *A History of Berwick-upon-Tweed* (1799)

Hallam, Jack, *Ghosts of the North* (David & Charles, 1976)

Hallowell, Michael J. & Ritson, Darren W., *Ghost Taverns* (Amberley, 2009)

Hallowell, Michael J., *Christmas Ghost Stories* (Amberley, 2009)

Hapgood, Sarah, *500 British Ghosts and Hauntings* (Foulsham, 1993)

Harries, John, *The Ghost Hunter's Road Book* (Letts, 1968)

Hippisley Coxe, Antony D., *Haunted Britain* (Pan, 1973)

Kirkup, Rob, *Ghostly Northumberland* (The History Press, 2008)

Lyndon Dodds, Glen, *Historic Sites of Northumberland and Newcastle-upon-Tyne* (Albion Press, 2002)

O'Donnell, Elliot, *Haunted Britain* (Rider, 1948)

O'Donnell, Elliot, *Scottish Ghost Stories* (Jarrold, 1981)

Price, Harry, *Poltergeist Over England* (Country Life Ltd, 1945)

Ritson, Darren W., *Haunted Newcastle* (The History Press, 2009)

Ritson, Darren W., *Ghost Hunter: True-Life Encounters from the North East* (GHP, 2006)

Ritson, Darren W., *In Search of Ghosts: Real Hauntings from Around Britain* (Amberley, 2008)

Ritson, Darren W., *Supernatural North* (Amberley, 2009)

Robson, Alan, *Grisly Trails and Ghostly Tales* (Virgin Books, 1992)

Underwood, Peter, *This Haunted Isle* (Harrap, 1984)

Underwood, Peter, *A Gazetteer of British Ghosts* (Souvenir Press, 1971)

Underwood, Peter, *The A-Z of British Ghosts* (Souvenir Press, 1971)

Picture Credits

Edward Longshanks (p17)
   http://en.wikipedia.org/wiki/File:Gal_nations_edward_i.jpg
Sawney Bean (p51)
   http://en.wikipedia.org/wiki/File:Sawney_beane.jpg
Vampire in grave (p55)
   http://en.wikipedia.org/wiki/File:Moraine_le_vampire.jpg

Berwick Castle and Breakneck Stairs, from the river's edge.

Other local titles published by The History Press

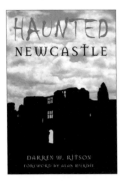

Haunted Newcastle
DARREN W. RITSON

This fascinating book contains over forty-five spine-chilling accounts from in and around central Newcastle. Take a tour of this ancient city and discover poltergeists, apparitions, curses, hauntings and even the ghost of a living person! From the ancient city walls to the cobbled back streets and chares of old Newcastle, and including graveyards, museums, stately halls, pubs, parks and monasteries, this book includes many pulse-raising narratives that are guaranteed to make your blood run cold.

978 0 7524 4880 0

Haunted Durham
DARREN W. RITSON

Haunted Durham contains a startling collection of true-life tales from in and around the city. From Durham Castle to Jimmy Allen's public house, discover poltergeists, hooded apparitions, headless horses, séances and exposed hoaxes. The author draws on historical and contemporary sources, and even shares his personal experiences of overnight surveillance with the paranormal investigation team GHOST. Containing many tales which have never before been published – including the crooked spectre of North Bailey and the ghost who bruised a barmaid's backside – this book will delight everyone interested in the paranormal.

978 0 7524 5410 8

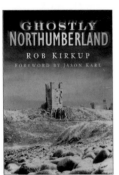

Ghostly Northumberland
ROB KIRKUP

Ghostly Northumberland investigates twenty of the most haunted locations in Northumberland today. Drawing on historical and contemporary sources, it includes a piano-playing ghost at Bamburgh Castle, the White Lady of Cresswell Tower, a mischievous poltergeist at the Schooner Hotel, as well as sightings of torturer John Sage, who continues to stalk the dungeons at Chillingham Castle – widely regarded to be one of the most haunted places in Britain. This book will appeal to everyone interested in finding out more about the county's haunted heritage.

978 0 7509 5043 5

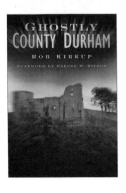

Ghostly County Durham
ROB KIRKUP

Ghostly County Durham investigates over twenty of the most haunted locations in the area today. Drawing on historical and contemporary sources, this selection includes a club-footed monk at Finchdale Priory, the 'Singing Lady' of Cauldron Snout, as well as a collection of spectres that call Durham Castle home –including a shadowy figure which haunts the Black Staircase.

978 0 7509 5124 1

Visit our website and discover thousands of other History Press books.

www.thehistorypress.co.uk